The Message of Romans

An Exposition

The Message of Romans

An Exposition

Robert C. McQuilkin

Columbia International University

Columbia, South Carolina

The Message of Romans: An Exposition

Updated edition
Copyright © 2015 by Columbia International University

7435 Monticello Rd.
Columbia, SC 29203
www.ciu.edu

Columbia International University educates people from a biblical
worldview to impact the nations with the message of Christ.

Editing, Cover and interior book design by Kelly Smith, Tallgrass Media.
Cover photo from pixabay.com, Creative Commons Public Domain (CC0).

Scripture quotations are from The Holy Bible, English Standard Version®
(ESV®), copyright © 2001 by Crossway, a publishing ministry of Good News
Publishers. Used by permission. All rights reserved.

First Printing: 1947

ISBN-13: 978-1-939074-06-5

Contents

Introduction to the Series

Dr. Robert C. McQuilkin served as the first president of Columbia International University, then named Columbia Bible College (CBC) for 29 years; 1923-1952. He served Christ and the Church as a magazine editor, a dynamic speaker, and a prolific writer. But he also had a deep passion to teach. During his tenure as president, he taught Romans, John, Daniel and Revelation, Progress of Doctrine, Hermeneutics and other courses. The books in this series spilled over from those courses and from popular sermons he preached across the nation.

Dr. McQuilkin expressed the vision for a biblical university that outlines my own service as president: "Neither a Bible institute nor a liberal arts college, Columbia Bible College offers a curriculum with the spiritual advantages of the former, and the cultural advantages of the latter."

After Dr. McQuilkin's sudden death, G. Allen Fleece led the school in its move to CIU's present location. His plans for expansion laid the foundation for Dr. McQuilkin's son, Robertson, who became president in 1968 when Dr. Fleece returned to his first love of evangelism.

Robertson McQuilkin left the church planting work he loved in Japan to lead CIU from 1968 to 1990. Robertson, like his dad, writes, preaches, and teaches. His books on hermeneutics, world evangelization, ethics, and the Holy Spirit continue in print and are used by schools and ministries around the world.

I invite you to join us in revisiting our rich heritage of the written works of Robert and Robertson McQuilkin. After all, together they provided leadership to CIU for over 50 years.

Within their writings, you will notice themes that form CIU's core values:

- Biblical Authority: The authority of Scripture as the defining rule for belief and practice.
- Victorious Christian Life: The victory in Christ that every Christian can experience through the filling of the Spirit.
- Prayer and Faith: The consistent practice by every Christian of personal witness to God's saving work in Christ.
- World Evangelization: The alignment of every Christian with God's heart for those around the world who have never heard the gospel.
- Evangelical Unity: Protecting the core truths of the faith, while seeking evangelical unity on all nonessentials.

We still live by these five core values as a school and to revisit them again in these books solidifies our commitment to them. We look back to remember and to underscore the importance of remaining tethered to our foundations, while exercising relevance in a dynamic, global community.

We look forward, until Christ returns, to serving His church by educating people from a biblical worldview to impact the nations with the message of Christ.

Dr. Bill Jones
President, Columbia International University
www.ciu.edu

Foreword

Why re-publish the writings of one who died more than a half century ago? Well, some would say, because they are classics by a major Christian author. But there's more.

Ninety years after their founding, very few institutions accurately reflect all the core values the founder held. But the grace of God through the creative genius of my father, Robert C. McQuilkin, has done just that. He was involved with initiating many movements and institutions. Some have morphed into something different than he envisioned. Some have disappeared. But the institution he poured his life into — Columbia Bible College — continues to this day in the vision and path he laid down, known today as Columbia International University.

Perhaps the enduring impact of his writing results in part, not only for its biblical fidelity on the God-intended life, but because his writing was signed and sealed by the life of the author. As I testified at his memorial service in 1952, "I know my father has sinned because 'all have sinned.' But I want you to know that for 25 years living in his house, I've never known him to fail."

It is fitting that this treasure trove should once again be made available to the CIU family and, as in the beginning, far beyond.

J. Robertson McQuilkin
President Emeritus
Columbia International University

Photo of Robertson McQuilkin with his father in the 1950s.

Original Dedication

To Marguerite Lambie McQuilkin
Life Partner in Bible Study
and Christian Living.

*Robert C. McQuilkin teaching Romans to a class at Columbia Bible
College (now Columbia International University) in the early 1950s.*

Original Foreword by the Author

Paul's letter to the Romans has influenced the world more than any other letter ever written. In this remarkable "book" the greatest questions of human life and destiny are discussed and answered.

Who is God, and how does He deal with men? Who is Jesus Christ, and what does He do for men? Who is the Holy Spirit, and how does He work in men? What is sin, and what is its result in men and in nations? Why are men lost? What is God's way of saving men? What is grace? What is Christian faith? What is the Church? What happens to those who have never heard of Christ? What happens to the Jews who do not accept Christ? What is the future destiny of the Jews, and of the whole human race? What happens to a man when he is saved? What is the relation of a Christian to the present world, to governments, to other Christians, to the Old Testament law, to doubtful questions of conduct, to sin? What is God's standard for Christian living? Can a Christian be sinless in this life? What is the secret of victory? What is God's missionary plan for the world?

These and other questions are answered in Paul's letter to the Romans. Yet the entire text could be printed on one page of a newspaper, and it can be easily read through in one sitting. It is a real letter, warm, personal, intimate and loving, aglow with the life-giving Spirit.

The purpose of this exposition is to help Christians "dig into" Romans for themselves, to enter into its inner spirit, to know the message and have it translated into life. It is hoped that these pages may help some to a new understanding of God's abounding grace that provides power to walk in newness of life.

Preparation for Lesson 1

If this book is used as a textbook for classes studying Romans, it will be well for the teacher to assign questions to be studied before the class period and before the text is read. The teacher may modify these assignments or frame her own questions and may add review questions at the end of each lesson. The material may be covered in these twelve lessons or in a longer or shorter course.

1. Read the first eleven chapters of the letter to the Romans at one sitting. The entire letter of sixteen chapters can be read rapidly aloud in thirty-five or forty minutes, so that a rapid reading without stopping to study may be done in thirty minutes, or in forty-five for slower readers. If interrupted in reading straight through, make a note of how many chapters you read at one sitting.

2. *The Outline.* Romans may be outlined in four main divisions. Without referring to any other outline, give what you think are good titles to describe the contents of the following chapters:
   A. 1:1–1:17
   B. 1:18–11:36
   C. 12:1–15:13
   D. 15:14–16:27

3. *The Greeting Paragraph.* Read again verses 1 to 7. Imagining that you have no knowledge of the Bible, read the verse as from a slip of paper. Write the things you would learn from this introduction. What central facts in these verses would stand out?

4. *Introduction to Romans* (1:1-17). After reading the Bible text, do you have a clear idea of the time, the occasion, the place, the readers and the relation of the book to the rest of the Bible? If not, review these and other introductory facts.

5. *The Theme and the Key Verses* (1:16-17). What is the theme of Romans? Why are 1:16-17 good key verses?

Lesson 1

Introduction to Romans

The Writer of the Letter: "Paul, a servant of Christ Jesus, called to be an apostle, set apart for the gospel of God."

In the Acts of the Apostles we have already been introduced to Paul, whose name is the first word in thirteen books of the Bible. Peter and John, the two chief apostles, were chosen of the Holy Spirit to write letters for the New Testament, and this was quite fitting. Two brothers of the Lord, James and Jude, were chosen to write part of the inspired Word. All of these men had known the Lord Jesus in the flesh. How remarkable it is that the Spirit should have committed to Paul, one who had never known Christ in the flesh, the writing of the thirteen letters, and probably Hebrews also, to set forth the Christian message. We can see how eminently Paul was qualified for this because of his own experience with Judaism, and his experience with the living Christ. He was trained in the learning of his day and knew Greek philosophy and Greek culture, and had a mind that has been recognized even by unbelievers as one of the greatest in all of history. Along with a keen intellect, he had a loving, tender heart, a deep humility and an experience of fellowshipping in the sufferings of Christ. But Romans is not Paul's view of the Gospel, the product of his own mind and heart. Romans is Christ's revelation through Paul.

Luke gave us a record of what Christ began to do and to teach. Then in Acts he gave us the record of what the risen, glorified Lord continued to do by the Holy Spirit, using His disciples. In the Epistles we have the record of what Christ has continued to teach, in completing

His Gospel message. He does it by the Spirit, and He does it by choosing as the chief instrument this Hebrew of the Hebrews who was the Apostle to the Gentiles.

The Readers: "To all those in Rome who are loved by God and called to be saints:" ...also "called Jesus Christ's." There is special significance in a letter sent to Rome, the center of the great world empire in which this little sect, which the Jews in Rome told Paul was everywhere spoken against, is to become the dominant force. Some scholars hold that the great majority in the church at Rome were Gentiles; others argue that Jews including proselytes were in the majority. In either case Gentile and Jewish elements in the Church were both very strong, and this determines the method of handling his message to them. It seems clear that Christianity was not established in Rome by any of the apostles. The "visitors from Rome, both Jews and proselytes" (Acts 2:10), who were present at Jerusalem on Pentecost, probably brought back to Rome the Good News concerning Christ. Other Christians may have had a part also, among them converts of Paul's. This letter was probably the first direct apostolic link with this work of the Spirit in the world's capital.

The Date of the Letter and the Place of Writing: Paul was in Corinth preparing to go to Jerusalem, previous to an expected visit to Rome. Read the following Scriptures, in order, writing down the facts given in each, and it will afford an interesting study showing just where Paul was when he wrote this letter: Rom. 1:11, 13, 15; 15:23-28; Acts 19:21 Rom. 15:26, 31; Acts 24:17; Rom. 16:21, 23; 1 Cor. 1:14; Acts 19:22; 1 Cor. 16:10-11; Acts 20:4; Rom. 16:1.

The letter was written at the close of his third missionary journey, the dates of which are variously given by eminent scholars. Several agree on 56-58, and we shall not be far wrong if we fix 58 A.D. as the date for Romans, between two or three years before he came to Rome as a prisoner, and perhaps about ten years before his death as a martyr.

The Occasion of the Letter, and Its Bearer: The verses noted in the paragraph above indicate the occasion of the letter. Paul is eager to visit Rome that he might impart some spiritual gift, to the end that they may be established (1:11). He has been hindered many times in this purpose, but now after he visits Jerusalem he plans to carry the message west into Spain, and visit Rome on the way (15:22-26).

As Paul completed dictating the the letter to Tertius in Corinth, Phoebe, a deaconess of the Church at Cenchrea, the eastern port of Corinth, was leaving for a visit to Rome on some business. She was likely the bearer of the letter to the believers in Rome (16:1-2, 22).

The occasion suggests the purpose also, though this lies much deeper than the immediate occasion. Paul does not merely want to send them a statement of his teaching in advance of his visit, but he also desires to make known to the Christians in Rome and throughout the world, just what is the Gospel of Grace and its relation to the old order. And all of this is to the end that they might know Christ personally and be established in Grace.

A feature of all of Paul's letters is the remarkable yet perfectly natural way in which each one was called forth by the circumstances of his ministry. He did not write the letters as part of a "New Testament." They leaped from his soul in the midst of his crowded ministry, as the vital, pressing needs of his spiritual children called them forth. Hence they are intensely practical, and intensely human. A study of the historical setting of the letters should give us a vivid appreciation of how real and personal these writings are. And it will add to our wonder and thanksgiving for the marvelous working of the Spirit who guided Paul's ministry through word and through pen to the end that these letters might also give the needed message for the Church in all ages.

Theme and Key Verses

The theme of Romans may be stated as *Paul's Gospel—Salvation by Grace through Faith in Jesus Christ.*

From the days of the great Protestant Reformation it has been customary to speak of "justification by faith" as the central theme of Romans. Justification by faith is indeed the foundation of the Christian message. Romans does set forth clearly that foundation doctrine. But the message of Romans does not stop with "justification." It goes on to present "sanctification" and "glorification." It presents salvation begun, salvation continued, salvation completed—and all by grace through faith. We may, therefore, state the theme as "salvation by grace through faith in Jesus Christ."

The theme of the Letter and the point of view in treating it is so clearly stated in Romans 1:16-17 that these two verses may be taken as key verses, even though Paul does not formally state that they give his purpose, as does John in the last verse of the twentieth chapter of his Gospel:

"For I am not ashamed of the gospel, for it is the power of God for salvation to everyone who believes, to the Jew first and also to the Greek. For in it the righteousness of God is revealed from faith for faith, as it is written, 'The righteous shall live by faith.'"

This message that Paul has is good news. When he says he is not ashamed of it, he is using a figure of speech to indicate that he rejoices in that Gospel with exceeding great joy. We are conscious in a new way in our day of what physical "power" means. We have used this Greek word for power to name the substance that used to be a synonym for mighty power; it was called dynamite. But atomic power has made dynamite in all its forms to be a rather mild form of physical energy. Yet none of this physical power wrapped up in God's creation can compare with the power needed to save a soul from sin and death. This is the grand and glorious message that Paul is bringing. He is going to reveal a righteousness of God. That is what man needs—righteousness. That is what he does not have. This expression does not refer to "the righteousness of God" in the sense of the righteous character of God. Paul is to tell of a righteousness which God has worked out for us, and which is to be presented as a free gift to everyone who believes. It is a righteousness by faith, beginning or springing out of faith, and going on in faith. Therefore, God's righteous man is the one who lives by faith, and no one else is righteous.

Paul says that this Gospel is "to the Jew first, and also to the Greek," or to the Gentile. This does not mean that wherever we go we should seek out all the Jews and preach the Gospel first to them (though this might be a wise procedure in some cases to offset the common neglect of the Jews). God's way of saving men is to take the message to all the Gentiles through the Jews, even as our Lord Jesus Himself came out of Israel. It comes to the Jew first in order that through the Jew the Gospel might go to all nations on earth. Our Lord told us plainly, "Salvation is from the Jews" (John 4:22).

The theme verses present not only the theme but Paul's viewpoint in treating the theme. He is to show the relationship between the Jew and Gentile. He is to present the meaning of law and grace, and the future of Israel. In doing this Paul will not be dealing with problems of his own day that have no bearing on our practical lives today. For these questions of law and grace, of sin and salvation, of God's way of righteousness, are the eternal questions that concern us today.

Yet deeper than all this, and giving meaning to it all, is the Lord Jesus Christ Himself, and His relation to the individual human soul. Christ Himself is Paul's theme and Paul's passion. To bring his reader into personal, vital union with Jesus Christ, His Lord—this is Paul's great objective.

Summary Outline of Romans

A. Greeting and Opening Personal Messages—1:1–1:17

Introducing the writer, the readers, and the subject: "For I long to see you, that I may impart to you some spiritual gift to strengthen you."

B. God's Way of Saving Men—1:18–11:36

1. *Sin Abounding in Jew and Gentile*—1:18–3:20

Revelation of God's wrath against sin.

The whole world needs a Saviour.

Key verse: 3:23.

2. *Grace Abounding for the Lost Sinner*—3:21–5:21

Revelation of God's righteousness.

Jew and Gentile both saved by grace through faith.

Key verses: 4:16 and 6:23.

3. *Grace Abounding for the Saint*—6:1–8:39

The saved man is to live under grace, by faith.

Key verses: 6:4; 8:4; 8:37.

4. *Grace Abounding for the World*—9:1–11:36

C. Exhortation to True Christian Living—12:1–15:13

In view of this salvation, live worthily, surrendering completely to Christ's control, shown in spiritual service and love for one another. Jew and Gentile were then dwelling together in unity. Key verses: 12:1-2.

D. Closing Personal Messages and Greeting—15:14 - 16:27

Paul's personal relation to them, his purpose to visit them, his personal salutations, and closing outburst of praise to the God of all Grace.

Key verses: 15:29 and 16:25.

Outline of Romans

God's way of saving men is set forth systematically in Romans as it is in no other portion of Scripture. Paul begins by proving that all men are lost, and step by step sets forth God's way of saving men, God's present and future provision for men after they are saved, and God's final plan for the world. It is the clear guidance of the Holy Spirit that after we learn of the establishing of the Church and the preaching of the Gospel in the Acts of the Apostles, we should have a letter that completely presents the meaning of the Christian faith. Appropriately it is the first of the New Testament letters.

Thus the nature of Paul's subject in Romans lends itself to a natural outline, and in a measure the book itself makes evident the definite plan the writer had in mind in arranging his material. We may, therefore, suggest a general outline that gives a true view of Romans, remembering that the message is a unit and the various divisions are not mechanically separated as in a modern textbook, but vitally joined the one to the other.

Romans is a true letter, and so it opens and closes with personal greetings (1:1-17 and 15:14 to 16:27). Paul's greetings can never be formal, and since to him Christ is the center of everything, it is most natural for him to link every bit of news or personal comment with a great message that is on his heart. What we may call the body of the letter falls into two natural divisions, the first eleven chapters telling in logical order the story of salvation by grace in its bearing on the past, present and future; the second division, beginning with the first verse of the twelfth chapter, "I appeal to you therefore, brothers," to surrender yourselves completely to this God of all grace and mercy, contains

Paul's personal exhortation to them in view of this great salvation.

Some teachers regard chapters 9 to 11 as a "parenthesis" in the argument, designed to show the relation of Israel to the Gospel. Paul is much given to parentheses, yet they are always vital to his central thought even when, to our way of thinking, they interrupt the logical flow of the reasoning. In the case of Romans 9 to 11, however, we are considering them in the present outline not as a parenthesis but as a glorious climax to the whole setting forth of God's way of saving men. They give God's missionary plan for the whole world, the plan He had in mind from the very beginning. They are indeed intended to make clear the relation of Israel to the Gospel, but this need not be a parenthesis, for we have seen how closely linked that subject is with his whole argument.

It would seem, then, a fair interpretation of Paul's own thought to divide this main section of the letter into the four parts suggested in the outline: Sin abounding, Grace abounding for the sinner, Grace abounding for the saint, Grace abounding for the world.

With these broad outlines of the letter before us, it will be well not to make a hard and fast division into sub-topics, but rather indicate in a suggestive way the contents and message under each general head. Each student or teacher may then modify the outline as seems best for his own needs.

Greeting and Opening Messages

Romans 1:1-17

INTRODUCTION: THE WRITER, THE READERS AND THEIR LORD—1:1-7

The remarkable paragraph with which the letter to the Romans opens may be better appreciated if we imagine that some person in Africa or China who has never heard of Christianity or the Bible has picked up a piece of paper with these seven verses clearly translated into her own language. There are more than twenty distinct and important things she could learn from that piece of paper. She would recognize it as part of a letter written by a man named Paul, to certain people in Rome called "saints." You may be sure she would be eager to see the rest of the letter, and also to get those "holy scriptures," or "sacred writings," that foretold the good news of the wonderful Person who has the central place in the paragraph.

The Person, "Jesus Christ our Lord," is a human being, descended from a man named David, yet He is called God's Son, and He is revealed as the Son of God by the miracle of the resurrection from the dead. Paul, the writer, is the servant of this wonderful Lord, and he is sent by God as an apostle to present Jesus Christ to all the nations, who are called on to believe this good news. Think what these things would mean to a spiritually hungry non-believer, such as the Japanese Neesima was, when he picked up a portion of the New Testament that had been washed up on the seashore. He became a servant of Jesus, transformed by grace divine, and then an apostle to his own people.

So the word "introduction" seems cold and formal as a designation for these glowing words, which sum up the message of the letter, all centering in the good news concerning Jesus Christ as Saviour and Lord.

PAUL'S PERSONAL RELATION, AND OCCASION OF THE LETTER—1:8-15

How tactful and loving is Paul's approach, enthusiastic over their faith in the Lord, not wishing to lord it over them as an apostle, but to rejoice together over their common inheritance in Christ. The greatness of what the humblest Christian shares with the chief apostle far surpasses the difference in authority and gifts between the two.

Some have supposed that Paul wished to bring to the saints at Rome a special gift in addition to what they had received. It is true that he was purposing to bring good news to them, and to let them realize the fullness and richness of their salvation. In this letter to them he is going to set forth the meaning of the marvels of the grace of God which already belonged to them as Christians. The letter would thus be a preparation for his visit to them.

What a remarkable testimony to faithfulness in prayer! Unceasingly he made mention of them. He loved them and yearned for them. His prayer that he might be enabled by the will of God to come to them was eventually answered. When the answer came, there was a shipwreck and suffering and danger of death. Some have said that this was not a prosperous journey. But Paul was enabled by the will of God to go to Rome, in God's time and in God's way. The Roman Empire paid the expenses of the trip, and there is no doubt that Paul was glad for all the experiences of the shipwreck.

Many missionaries have gotten a thrilling message from Paul's "I am debtor…I am ready." It was a message for the two great classes of Gentiles—the Greeks, and the others they called Barbarians, not meaning barbarous people but simply foreigners, those who were non-Hellenic or non-Roman.

THE SUBJECT STATED IN THE KEY VERSES—1:16-17

"As it is written, 'The righteous shall live by faith.'" How significant this first quotation from the Old Testament. This new Gospel Paul preaches is new *and old*. The text that Paul is taking for this presentation of the message of the New Dispensation is a text from the Old Testament. He is to tell the Jews that he is not bringing something different from the revelation which God gave from the beginning. The Old Testament preached righteousness by faith. It is the heart of the Old Testament message as of the New. From the moment that sin entered the world everyone who has been saved has been saved by grace through faith. This quotation sums up the whole of the message: righteousness, life and faith—these three can never be separated.

This remarkable sentence from Habakkuk 2:4: "The righteous shall live by faith," is quoted three times in the New Testament: Romans 1:17, Galatians 3:11, Hebrews 10:38. Dr. William J. Erdman and others have suggested that each time there is a different emphasis. In Romans: "But the *righteous* shall live by his faith." In Galatians: "The righteous shall live by *faith*." In Hebrews: "The righteous shall *live* by faith."

Preparation for Lesson 2

Reading Lesson: Romans 1-3

For Special Study: Romans 1:18–3:20

1. Write in your notebook an explanation of the two things that those who have never heard about about God would know because of the revelation of nature. Explain this in terms of the statements in Romans and also in terms of the present-day knowledge of the unreached.

2. What other revelations of God do they have?

3. Sum up in your own words the main argument of Paul from Romans 1:18 to the end of chapter 1. Why are those who have never heard of Christ lost?

4. Sum up the argument of Paul in chapter 2. What classes of sinners does Paul deal with in this chapter?

5. What does the goodness of God leading to repentance mean? Who are described in 2:7? What does 2:13 mean?

6. Sum up the teachings of Romans 3:1-20. In what way are Jews and Gentiles brought together in this statement? Does the terrible description in 3:10-18 apply to all? If so, in what sense?

Lesson 2

God's Way of Saving Men

Romans 1:18-11:36

SIN ABOUNDING IN JEW AND GENTILE—1:18-3:20

Revelation of God's Wrath Against Sin
The Whole World Needs a Saviour: "All have sinned" (Rom. 3:23).

In Romans there is a sad story and a glad story. The sad story is sin abounding. The glad story is Grace abounding, the Gospel, the "so great salvation." If we have a "so great salvation," it must be a deliverance from very great sin and danger. The first page of the Gospel story must, therefore, be the story of sin abounding. Paul's first concern is to prove that all men are lost, because God's salvation through Christ is provided only for lost men who cannot save themselves. This first section in the story of salvation proves that "all have sinned, and fall short of the glory of God" (3:23). Paul proves as to Jew and Gentile that "they are all under sin" (3:9).

In treating this subject Paul has before him the two classes—Jews and Gentiles. Jews, of course, include proselytes—Gentiles who have accepted the true and living God (whether from the heart or merely outwardly), and have been circumcised. The Jews are they who have the revelation of God. The Gentiles are the nations that do not have this revelation. Paul must show that both Jews and Gentiles are under sin, and that they have no excuse. He must show that those who have never heard of the Saviour, and have never had a revelation of God, are nevertheless in sin, and lost. He must show also that the Jews may know exactly what God has told them to do, and yet they are lost because they have not done it.

1. GENTILES, WHO HAVE THE REVELATION OF NATURE, HAVE REJECTED THEIR LIGHT AND ARE LOST—1:18-32

He begins, "For the wrath of God is revealed from heaven against all ungodliness and unrighteousness of men." An ungodly man is not necessarily the blatant infidel. He is the man who lives his life without reference to God. America is full of ungodly people. God is not in all their thoughts, even though many of them may be conforming to the outward moral standards of their community. Unrighteousness is anything contrary to the righteous standards of God. The phrase "who by their unrighteousness suppress the truth" may mean either to possess the truth and yet be unrighteous, or to throttle the truth by their unrighteousness. In either case there is the dread truth of God's wrath upon all men who are contrary to the truth.

He proceeds to show that they are without excuse, and he is speaking here not of Jews but of Gentiles. They have the revelation of nature. Through God's creation they know two things about God. They know His eternal power. A man cannot create a blade of grass. What must be the power of One who can create the universe, including man? They know also His deity. He must be different from men. We are human; He must be divine. Knowing these two things, a man knows that he should worship God. But men have turned away from God. Paul is speaking here both of the original turning from God and the present condition of the heathen world. There are twin sins—idolatry and immorality. There is a fearful list of twenty-one sins at the close of this first chapter. These sins are the natural outcome of turning from the truth of God to an error. Not all men have gone so far into outward corruption, but these things are the fruit of that first sin.

We shall not need to use imagination to gather the effect of this section upon those who have never heard of Christ. Some years ago the author was in a little group that was discussing conditions in the mission field, following an address by a missionary from Africa at America's Keswick. The missionary related his interesting experience in translating the New Testament. When he came to the first chapter of Romans, the young Africans who were helping him with his translating appeared much embarrassed, and one by one they got up and left. One of the leaders, a young man close to the missionary, explained to him afterward that they considered he had not treated them fairly in coming into their country, getting their confidence, learning all their ways, and then writing what he knew about them in a book for everyone to read.

In this group listening to the missionary from Africa was a former missionary of the China Inland Mission, and he told the experience of Hudson Taylor when he was translating the New Testament, assisted by a group of China's cultured literati. When they came to the first chapter of Romans, Dr. Taylor noticed a strange reticence. He could get little help from them, and one after another excused himself, leaving the missionary alone and puzzled. Soon after, one of the men confidentially explained to Dr. Taylor that these scholars were much offended that the missionary should be guilty of such a breach of good taste. Coming as a foreigner to their country, gaining their confidence, seeing the inner conditions of things that were hidden from the ordinary traveler, he writes a description of it and reads it as part of an ancient book.

Heathenism is the same in Rome and Corinth, in pagan Africa and in civilized China, among the ignorant Barbarians and the cultured Greeks. Paul does not mean that every man who rejects God is living this low, vile life. He does mean that every man whose sin is not taken away, eventually and inevitably will go into complete corruption, as the unchecked cancer will finally eat out the whole physical life.

All men know in their hearts that there is a God. Philosophers argue the question whether this knowledge is intuitive. The fact remains that people from every culture and ethnic group know in their heart that there is one God who is over all. Dan Crawford, the famous missionary to Africa once declared: "The natives in the heart of Africa, who have never heard of Christ, are sinning against a flood of light." Crawford asked a native chief: "Do you believe in one great God?" The answer was, "No rain, no mushrooms; no God, no world." Of course, he knew that there was a God, and that God is the Creator. And that is the knowledge God will hold him responsible for. The light the Gentiles have, Paul says, is that God is the Creator; this light they turn from, and serve the creature rather than the Creator. This is turning from the truth to the lie. The final, ultimate human religion is the worship of man as God. Man's religion, when its course is run, will end where it began, for the father of lies uses the same lie to turn men away from the One who is the Truth.

But the Gentiles not only have the light that comes from nature. All men have the revelation of conscience. Strictly speaking, "conscience" does not tell a man what is right. Conscience is the witness within a man's heart that there is a difference between right and wrong, and conscience tells him to do the thing that is right. So when he does what he considers wrong, we say that his conscience hurts. Men also have the original revelation passed down through Noah and his sons,

Shem, Ham and Japheth. There are remarkable evidences among various tribes in Africa that they have had knowledge of Old Testament revelations of God. J. Alexander Clark and Norman Davis of the Sudan Interior Mission, made lists of names of God found among the tribes in Central Africa and in Nigeria. Many of the Old Testament names of God were found in these languages: "The-One-who-is-from-ever-lasting-to-everlasting"; "The-breasted-One"; "The-One-with-Whom-you-cannot-lay-a-bet," that is, the sovereign God; "The-One-Who-blesses-indiscriminately-here-but-separates-for-blessing-hereafter."

Thus clearly does Romans answer that oft-repeated and foolish question as to how God can fairly condemn men who have never heard of Christ, when they do not know God. The answer is that they do know God. They are not condemned for rejecting a Saviour of whom they have never heard. They are condemned for sinning against the light they have.

But there follows the next question, "If a man lives up to the light that he has, will he not be saved, though he has not heard of Christ?" The answer to this is to ask another question: "How many men and women in your community live up to the light they have for a single day?" A clear revelation of God's Word, confirmed by our own experience, is that since sin entered the world no man has ever lived up to the light that he has, with the one exception of our Lord Jesus Christ. That is why men are lost. That is why they must be saved by grace through faith. Romans proves the truth of what our Lord Himself distinctly taught: "I am the way, and the truth, and the life: no one comes to the Father, except through me" (John 14:6). We cannot revise this to read, "no one comes to the Father, except through me, with the exception of the heathen who have never heard of me."

There is one thing that the heathen can do about his sin. He can recognize that he is not living up to his light, and that he needs a Saviour. We have frequent instances of men in heathen lands who have thrown away their idols and have prayed to the true God. God answers that prayer in just one way and that is, somehow to bring the good news of Christ to that soul.

Dr. Charles Ernest Scott, veteran missionary statesman of China, years ago told this incident of his first term of service in China. He went with a visitor from America to a mountain village in China that had never been visited by white men. When they came to that village they heard that there was a Black Night Society. This name sounded a bit ominous. They discovered that the men of that village met at night and conferred together about the true God who had created the heavens and the earth. The Elders in the village had destroyed every idol, because they recognized that the true God was the Creator. The missionary found that the people in that little village were fascinated as they sat and heard the story about the true and living God, whom they recognized as the One to be worshiped. There was an amazing openness for the message and some of them turned in faith to that Saviour who was presented.

But suppose the missionary had not gone? This brings before us a picture of a football field at the University of Pennsylvania. It was during the years when the University of Pennsylvania had a championship football team. One of the players was a brilliant young student who was planning to go to the foreign mission field. His friends told him he would be wasting his talents. He went into work among the lumbermen in the United States and had such success that he was told that he should continue serving the Lord at home. But the call was to China. The God who heard the heart cry of those Chinese in the little mountain village in China who had destroyed their idols and were calling out for light to the true God, this Lord of the Harvest called Charles Ernest Scott. If he had turned back from the call doubtless God would have chosen someone else. But he did not turn back. May we not conclude that wherever men call upon God He answers that prayer in sending to them the messenger who will give good news concerning Christ. So in a later chapter Paul gives the wonderful news, "Everyone who calls on the name of the Lord will be saved," and adds these searching questions: "How then will they call on him in whom they have not believed? And how are they to believe in him of whom they have never heard? And how are they to hear without someone preaching? And how are they to preach unless they are sent? As it is written, 'How beautiful are the feet of those who preach the good news!'"

Dr. Roland V. Bingham, pioneer missionary in Africa, and for many years the beloved leader of the Sudan Interior Mission, gathered illustrations of this very truth. He prepared a book on the subject, but it was not published at the time of his death. Mrs. Bingham kindly sent a copy of the chapter on "How a Governor in Siam Found Christ," and gave permission for its publication. The following is a condensation of this remarkable narrative:

"Down in the Malay Peninsula a Christian missionary was preaching the Gospel to the multitudes who gathered to hear his message... For more than thirty years he has been a missionary in that country, and he loves the blessed work of traveling over the various provinces on long itineraries often lasting six months. When I saw him in his home in Bangkok he was just starting on a journey of this sort. From his lips I heard the following story:

"Some years ago he was in the Malay Peninsula in a region where he had never been before, and was very much surprised to hear that the governor of that province believed in Christ. He inquired if any missionary had ever been there and was told that no preacher had ever visited the place, but once a man was there selling copies of a book. The governor heard of this book and bought one of the volumes. Now, the teachings of this book, according to the report that came to the missionary, were very like his preaching. He expressed a desire to see the governor and was told that the messenger had gone to announce the stranger's coming. Soon he received a request to visit the place, which he did, accompanied by his wife.

"As they entered the beautiful grounds about the palace, they saw through the trees an old man with a gray beard, clad in white, standing on the verandah of the house, and by his side in white, stood his wife. When they caught sight of the approaching visitors they exclaimed: 'Hosanna! Hosanna!' When they were all seated together on the verandah, the old man told of their remarkable experience. Thirty years before, when he and his wife were one day mending some of the broken idols, he suddenly stopped and called her attention to the wonderful character of the human hand, capable of making so many things. He said that his hand was a greater thing than these lifeless images they were mending. Then he declared that human beings, intelligent and creative, were greater than these pieces of wood and stone that they shaped into images and worshiped. 'How absurd it is for us to worship these dead things, as if they could do anything for us!' he exclaimed. His wife agreed with him, saying that she had often thought the same thing.

"They decided that they would worship these creatures of their own hands no longer, but would destroy them. This they did and returned to the empty room from which they had taken the idols, wondering what they should worship now. The governor said to his wife: 'There must be a Being greater than man who made man and the earth and the stars. We will worship Him, the greatest Being in the universe.'

"The governor said that at last he heard of a man in his province who was selling a book. A sudden thrill of confidence came into his heart that this book was what he had waited for so long. In eager haste he sent for the man and asked for the book. The man said: 'This is the book that tells about the greatest Being in the universe.' With trembling hand the governor bought it. It was a copy of the Christian Scriptures translated into his own language. The old governor told the missionary how he and his wife sat on the verandah for many hours while he read to her the wonderful book from beginning to end. It was the Bread of Life to their starving souls.

"When the governor and his wife came to Paul's sermon to the Athenians on Mars Hill, where he spoke of the people worshiping the 'unknown God,' he said, 'Wife, we have been living in Athens for thirty years!' Through the word of God alone, without a human voice to help them, taught by the Holy Spirit of truth, they came to know the true God and Jesus Christ whom he has sent.

"When the governor ceased to worship idols, he told his people of his convictions and practices, but he could not tell them much about any other religious life. When he came to know his Bible, however, he became prepared to teach them and help them to know the truth and obey it. The people had asked him for a statement of his faith and he told the missionary that finally he had written it down. Going to a little box, he took from it his confession of faith and read it aloud. With keenest anticipation, the missionary listened to learn what a man thus taught of God only, would formulate as his creed. 'I believe in God, the Father of all things. I believe in Jesus Christ, the Son of God, as my Saviour. I believe in the Holy Ghost as my Comforter and

Teacher.' The statement contained the fundamental essentials of the faith that are accepted by the evangelical Christian church with no addition of false views.

"The missionary said farewell to the aged couple, telling them that he soon expected to go home to America to visit his parents. The governor looked appealing at his newly found Christian brother and said, 'Missionary, I am an old man and may not live until you come again, but I wish to ask one favor. When I die, I will go to heaven but I will be far back among the unworthy ones, for I have been an idolater and have done so little for my Lord. But you will be close to the throne, for you have had a long life of blessed service. Please promise me that you will tell Jesus that I would love to be allowed to come near Him just once that I may see His glory.' This man was the only person who had the right to present any of his people to the King, and he had not appreciated the difference between the kingdoms of earth and heaven in some of these things. Like a little child he believed and loved his Lord and in his humility he counted himself as one who would sit far down at the feast.

"With tears of joy they separated. More than a year later, the missionary visited the place again. The governor had gone to behold the King in His beauty, and to realize that he would not need any special introduction by any man."

Such experiences as these, which have been repeated many, many times, suggest that anywhere in the world when men recognize themselves as sinners and call upon God, He will see to it that the Gospel message gets to him. We have, of course, no way of knowing of anyone's calling on God to save him who has not had the message brought. However, it is significant that we have no instance of anyone having found salvation except through the written or spoken Word which presents Christ. There is no basis either in the Scripture or human experience for what is called "the larger hope," that is, that God may save many of the heathen apart from the knowledge of Christ, or that He may bring to the heathen that knowledge of Christ without the use of the human messenger, giving either the spoken or the written Word.

2. THE JEWS, WHO HAVE THE LAW, HAVE BROKEN THE LAW AND ARE LOST—2:1-29

In the second chapter Paul deals with those who condemn these sins of the Gentiles and yet are themselves sinners. Some consider that in the first sixteen verses Paul is dealing with moral Gentiles, and that beginning with verse 17 he deals with the Jews. Others believe that the Jew is included in the discussion of the whole chapter. In any case, the truth is clear. The Jew has the written law. But the Gentile also has the law written in his heart (2:14,15). God's judgment falls on men without respect to whether they are Gentiles or Jews. The Gentiles who sin without the law perish without the law, and the Jews who sin under the law are judged and condemned by the law (vs. 12). Paul is proclaiming the truth that made the Jews gnash their teeth in anger against him: "For it is not the hearers of the law who are righteous before God, but the doers of the law who will be justified"(vs. 13). Paul is not speaking about getting saved by the works of the law. He is not here discussing the plan of salvation by grace as opposed to the plan of trying to get saved by works. He is contrasting those who have heard the law and do not carry it out, and those who hear the law and by the grace of God do it (although not perfectly).

Paul tells those who condemn outward wickedness, and who believe they are favorites of God because of His mercy to them, that this goodness and forbearance and long-suffering of God is intended to lead them to repentance (vs. 4). There is coming that day of wrath and judgment. God will render to every man according to his works (vs. 5-6). Paul divides men into two classes—those who "by patience in well-doing seek for glory and honor and immortality," and those who are "self-seeking and do not obey the truth, but obey unrighteousness." To the one is given eternal life. To the other there is "there will be wrath and fury. There will be tribulation and distress for every human being who does evil, of the Jew first, and also the Greek" (2:6-9). This whole argument is to show that God essentially deals with Jew and Greek in exactly the same way (2:11). Those who by patient continuance in well-doing seek for glory and honor, are of course, those who have accepted Christ as their Saviour; they have been born of the Spirit and the evidence is their manner of life. The others are those who have rejected Christ, who do not obey the truth.

It throws everything into confusion to suppose that Paul is dealing with salvation by works. Some have gone so far as to teach that God has two plans of salvation. They say that God did desire to save men by having them, by patience in well-doing seek for glory and honor and immortality. Since men did not do this, God sent Christ to die for them. This led to the teaching that the Cross was an afterthought in the mind of God. Not many go to this logical extreme, and yet they suppose that Paul is here speaking of being justified by works rather than by faith, and they call it a lower form of justification. All through the New Testament, and indeed all through the Bible, there is emphasized the principle that faith is proved by works, and therefore, judgment is according to works. But when they are justified by works, the works must always be the fruit of faith, springing from the grace of God, and not by "works of the law," which would be their own righteousness.

There follows in verses 17 to 29 an arraignment of the Jew, "For no one is a Jew who is merely one outwardly" (2:28). It is true that he belongs to the race by outward birth. Esau also was a son of Isaac after the flesh. But Paul says, "For circumcision indeed is of value if you obey the law" (2:25). He is not meaning that some were justified by doing the law. He is speaking of those who are true believers and who by God's grace are fulfilling the law, though no man has done this perfectly.

3. JEW AND GENTILE ALIKE ARE GUILTY AND UNDER THE JUDGMENT OF GOD—3:1-20

This discussion of Paul raises the question as to whether there is, after all, any difference between Jew and Gentile. The conclusion might be, there is no advantage in being a Jew (3:1). But Paul says, there is "much in every way" (3:2), and in the opening paragraphs of the third chapter he sums up the arguments, proving that both Jew and Gentile are under sin. Paul puts together statements from seven different passages in the Old Testament to prove that the Jew, and also all men, apart from salvation by grace through faith in Christ, are lost, without God and without hope. He concludes that all the world is under the judgment of God: "For by works of the law no human being will be justified in his sight, since through the law comes knowledge of sin" (3:20).

This is the black page. It is the dark picture. He has shown that sin abounds in two distinct ways. It abounds extensively. There is not one single human being omitted. All have sinned. This includes infants who do not live to the age of accountability. They have not sinned by their own choice. But as he proves later, they belong to a sinful race, and in Adam, the father of the race, they have sinned; moreover, they have inherited a sinful human nature. But sin abounds also intensively. Sin is abounding in every human heart. There are degrees of sin. As to the fact of sin, there is no degree. Not every man has gone into corruption, but every man will eventually go into corruption unless he is saved from his sin. If there were only one sinner in the world, that sin would require all the sacrifice of Christ on Calvary. Moreover, every human heart, apart from God's grace, is capable of the vilest sin ever committed by human beings.

Preparation for Lesson 3

Reading lesson: Romans 3:21–5:21; James 2:14-26; Galatians 3

1. What does Paul mean by God's "passing over of sins"? (3:23; cf. Acts 14:16-17; 17:30).

2. What is the meaning of Christ set forth as a propitiation (vs. 25)? Read Hebrews 9:5, 1 John 2:2 and 4:10.

3. Sum up the teaching of Paul in Romans 3:21-31. Can you get the connection between this teaching and all that goes before? How would you explain the connection between the justification apart from the works of the law in Romans 3:20, also in this passage 3:21-31, and the statement made in Romans 2:13, "The doers of the law shall be justified"?

4. Sum up briefly the argument of Paul in chapter 4. Notice that Abraham's faith was in the God "who gives life to the dead" (4:17). Our faith is in what (4:24)? Read Galatians 3:21 and notice the connection between God's power to make alive and the salvation that comes through faith. What was it that the law could not do? Why was it necessary to do that thing which the law could not do, in order to save us and to make us righteous?

5. Does James seem to be contradicting Paul when he says, "a person is justified by works and not by faith alone" (Jas. 2:24)? Notice that he uses Abraham as an example just as Paul does. He says of Abraham, "By works was faith made perfect." Does this mean, after all, that something was to be added to faith in order that a person might be saved?

6. What is the difference between works done under the law, before faith comes, and the works done under grace, after faith comes?

Lesson 3

Grace Abounding for the Lost Sinner

Romans 3:21-5:21

1. GOD'S WAY OF SAVING JEW AND GENTILE, BY GRACE THROUGH FAITH IN JESUS CHRIST, CRUCIFIED AND RISEN—3:21-31

Key Verses: 4:16 and 6:23

A new page is turned with those words "But now."

Some years ago the writer was sitting on the platform in the famous Sunday Morning Breakfast Association in Philadelphia. There were perhaps two hundred broken wrecks of humanity attending the Sunday morning meeting in the Rescue Mission. Many others were there who had come out of darkness into His marvelous light, and gave their testimonies. A fine-looking gentleman sitting with the choir on the platform rose to give his testimony. I judged that he was one of the workers from a city church. In a few words he sketched the story of how sin had taken him lower than the lowest of the wrecks of men who had come into the hall for bread and coffee. After describing what sin had done for him, with a glowing face he exclaimed, "But God—O glorious *but!*" It is a thrilling study to go through the New Testament and mark these glorious *buts* of the Gospel (cf. Eph. 2:1-3; Titus 3:3-5).

In the suggestive "Wordless Story," the first page is black: that is Romans 1:18-3:20. The next page is blood red, making possible the

35

changing of that black page to white: that is Romans 3:21-5:21.

Against that black picture of sin abounding, Paul is now giving the glorious message of a "righteousness of God." The wrath of God was revealed against all unrighteousness and ungodliness of men. Men need righteousness, and they do not have it. Now there is the revelation of a righteousness which God is to give to man.

The foundation and the heart of all Christian doctrine, justification by grace through faith, is set forth more definitively in these eleven verses that close the third chapter of Romans than in any other paragraph in the Bible. It is related of Dr. William G. Moorehead, the noted Bible teacher of the United Presbyterian Church, that he would always ask candidates for the ministry to explain this passage of Scripture. If the young man understood the teaching clearly, Dr. Moorehead would be in favor of his ordination, whatever his other failures might be. If he did not understand this message, Dr. Moorehead would not favor the ordination, however well qualified in other ways he might be.

The problem of all problems with regard to sin is: How can God clear the guilty? The answer is that God cannot clear the guilty, unless the penalty is fully paid. If God's plan of salvation by grace through faith made the law of none effect, God's righteousness would be destroyed, and there would be nothing in salvation. Paul says that by this plan the law is not done away, but rather established (3:31).

We are justified freely, Paul says, by God's grace (3:2-4), that is, we are declared righteous. The word "freely" is the same word that is used in the expression: "they hated me without a cause" (John 15:25). There was nothing in Christ to call forth hatred; they hated Him freely, or without cause. So with not the slightest righteousness in us, we who are unrighteous are declared righteous, by His grace. Grace means that God did it all. Instantly there follow the words "through the redemption." There was a price paid. And what a price! It was not "freely" in the sense that the gift cost God nothing. The Lord Jesus Christ was set forth "a propitiation" (3:25). This propitiation was "in his blood," which shows that he is speaking of the death on the Cross. The propitiation is the penalty for sin, the penalty for the broken law, and it is rendered to God. There is the mystery that God is the one who makes the sacrifice, and God is the one to whom the sacrifice is made. God was in Christ, reconciling the world to Himself. The sacrifice of the righteous one demonstrated that God could be righteous and yet forgive sin. It proved that when He "passed over" the sins done from Adam to the Cross, "the former sins" (3:25), it was not the ignoring of sin by God, but the righteous dealing with sin. He passed them over, not in the sense that men would not suffer for their sins. The wages of sin is death. But those who had faith had their sins forgiven. The nations who did not have faith were nevertheless given many blessings, and wrath and destruction were postponed. In other words, God has always dealt with sin from the time Adam and Eve sinned in the garden of Eden, on the ground of the blood of Christ. All the blessings that come to the human race, including the blessings upon those who do not have faith, come from God's grace through the Lord Jesus Christ.

Here then is the good news. God declares righteous everyone that has faith in Jesus, whether he is a circumcised Jew or an uncircumcised Gentile. The ground of this righteousness is the righteousness of Christ and His blood; but there is also a condition: the condition is faith.

This righteousness that Paul speaks of is not the righteous character of God. It was the righteousness that Christ wrought out for men by His incarnation, His sinless life, His observance of all the righteous requirements of God's law, His atoning death, His resurrection, His ascension to the right hand of power.

The practical message here is simple. When a man is convicted of sin, he knows that he is lost. He has broken the law of God. He may not have gone into terrible, outward sin. But he has come short of the glory of God. He has not loved God with his whole being, nor has he loved his neighbor as himself. A perfect keeping of these two commandments is the only righteousness that God can accept. The Lord Jesus Christ is the only human being who ever lived up to these commands, since sin entered the world. Paul is proving, therefore, that all are included in sin. There is no distinction between Jew and Gentile. None has measured up to God's requirement. The Jew has sinned against God's written law for him. The Gentile has sinned against God's written law in his heart, and written in nature. All have sinned against the light they have. There is no exception. The conscience of man, as well as the Word of God, tells him that he is a sinner, and that there is no possible way of justifying him, unless a way is found to pay the penalty of the sin. Paul has concluded his section of sin abounding by the words, "For by works of the law no human being will be justified in his sight, since through the law comes knowledge of sin" (3:20).

The law of God shows me that I am a lost sinner. If I could keep perfectly every requirement of the law from this moment on, it would not avail, for I have already broken the law. But I cannot keep the law perfectly, because I am a sinner. There is nothing we can do toward saving ourselves. It must come from God, and therefore, it must be of grace.

Here is One whom God sets forth a propitiation for sin. Later Paul will answer the objection that immediately arises, that if this is the plan, then men may freely go on sinning and still have the righteousness of Christ. But he makes clear that there is one condition. It is "through faith." The Gospel is the power of God not "to everyone" but "to everyone that believes." The righteousness of Christ is ever the ground of salvation for any sinner. His own faith is not the ground; his faith is a condition, and this faith also must come from God. The realization that Christ's righteousness is ours brings unspeakable joy to each one who apprehends it clearly. We are not merely pardoned sinners. We stand before God as though we had never sinned. This righteousness is absolutely perfect righteousness for the weakest saint, and for the greatest spiritual warrior.

2. SALVATION BY GRACE THROUGH FAITH IN THE OLD TESTAMENT—4:1-25

Paul is careful to explain to the Jews that salvation by grace through faith does not nullify the law. The Jews think that Paul is proclaiming a new thing. Therefore, he proceeds to show that Abraham and David, and all the saved people of the Old Testament, were saved by grace through faith. He makes clear that this is not a new revelation of God, but the original revelation, brought to clear light through the death and resurrection of Christ. This salvation has been "witnessed by the law and the prophets" (3:21).

It is a striking fact that the two great verses on which Paul bases his exposition of salvation by grace through faith are verses in the Old Testament: "Abraham believed God, and it was counted to him as righteousness" (4:3), quoted from Genesis 15:6, and "the righteous shall live by faith" (1:17), quoted from Habakkuk 2:4. Abraham is the pioneer of faith. He is the father of all those who have faith. Abraham was not counted righteous because of his works, but because of his faith in the God who gives righteousness to the ungodly. When it is said that Abraham's faith was reckoned for righteousness, it does not mean that Abraham's faith made him a good man, and that, therefore, it was counted to him as righteousness. In that case, we should need to look at Abraham to understand righteousness. There are those who think that when a man repents and turns from sin, and has faith in God, that changed attitude of his makes him a righteous man. But the very meaning of the word "faith" makes impossible such a conclusion. Faith points to another. When we think of Abraham justified by faith, we look not at Abraham, but we look at the righteousness of Christ. Abraham's faith is the instrument by which he takes hold of that righteousness. But the faith is not the righteousness. We can, of course, speak of faith that justifies; also, the blood of Christ justifies; but each in its own order, and in its own way.

There are some who teach that Abraham was saved by grace through faith, but that when the law came at Sinai the Jews were to be justified through the keeping of the law. Some say that the Jews mistakenly put themselves under law, and that God permitted them to do it. This mistake would not be made if we remember that Paul, immediately after speaking of Abraham, writes: "just as David also speaks of the blessing of the one to whom God counts righteousness apart from works" (4:6). Be it observed that David is not here speaking of himself, or some other special spiritual leader. He is speaking of any person whose iniquities are forgiven and whose sins are covered. Some would say that in the Old Testament the sins are just "covered," and not yet "done away." But the Word says, "Blessed is the man against whom the Lord will not count his sin." This means that every person in the Old Testament who was saved, was saved through the righteousness of Christ. There is only one justification, and that justification is perfect. It is on the ground of the perfect righteousness of Christ.

Then comes the question as to whether this great blessing is only for Jews, or for Gentiles also. This was a burning question at that time. Some believing Jews were insisting that Gentiles should be circumcised. Paul completely and yet very simply overthrows that argument. Abraham was counted righteous before he was circumcised. Then he was circumcised as "seal of the righteousness that he had by faith while he was still uncircumcised" (4:11). Thus, Abraham is the father of all uncircumcised people who believe. He is not the father of circumcised people who do not believe, but he is the father of those who are not only circumcised but who have that faith that Abraham had before he was circumcised (4:12).

Thus is the Gospel separated utterly from any connection with righteousness that comes from keeping the law. One of the great key verses that sums up the argument is 4:16: "That is why it depends on faith, in order that the promise may rest on grace." Faith excludes all boasting. When it is of faith, then it is according to grace. Grace means Jesus does it all for us. It follows that the promise is sure to Jews and Gentiles, all of whom are children of Abraham if they have faith (4:16).

God's promise to Abraham that he would have a son and that he would be a father of many nations, was not simply the promise of a child, such as married people might pray for today. This promise of Isaac was tied up with the whole plan of redemption. Abraham's faith in the Word of God, therefore, was a forerunner of the faith of everyone who takes Christ as Saviour. As Abraham believed for the miracle of the birth of Isaac, and later believed for the miracle for the resurrection of Isaac, so when we take Christ as our Saviour, we believe that He died for our sins and rose again: "who was delivered up for our trespasses and raised for our justification" (4:25).

Preparation for Lesson 4

Reading Lesson: Romans 5:1–7:6

Blessing of the Justified: Past, Present, Future (5:1-11)

1. List the several blessings that come to one who has believed in Christ. Are you enjoying all of them? If not, why not?

2. Study verse 1. What is the significance of "therefore"? What is the basis for the peace?

3. What does it mean to glory in tribulation? What reasons are given for rejoicing in tribulation?

4. What is the hope that puts not to shame? On what is it based? Is present victory promised? What is the "wrath" in verse 9?

Adam and Christ—Abounding Sin and Abounding Grace (5:12.31)

5. What does the first Adam stand for in contrast to Christ, "the last Adam"?

6. Do verses 18 and 19 seem to mean that as all are lost in Adam so all men universally will be saved through Christ? How would you explain this?

7. What difference was there in the time from Adam to Moses and from Moses to Christ? What is one purpose of the giving of the law under Moses?

8. How is the expression "much more" used in this chapter? Can it be taken as a key?

9. What assurance of victory in present life is given in these verses? What is the connection of chapter 6 with 5?

10. What doctrine regarding the reason for universal sin is given in this chapter? What are some wrong views on this subject?

Lesson 4

Grace Abounding for the Lost Sinner

(Part 2)

3. THE BLESSINGS OF THE JUSTIFIED—5:1-11

Let us get the wonder of Paul's great argument and apply it personally to our lives. He writes: "Therefore, since we have been justified by faith, we have peace with God through our Lord Jesus Christ" (5:1). Notice the "therefore." If we were justified or declared righteous in any other way than "by faith," we could not have perfect peace. Since we are justified by faith, it means that our justification rests not in anything in ourselves, not in our feelings, nor in our good works, but in the righteousness of our Lord Jesus Christ. Does the righteousness of Christ satisfy God the Father? That is what gives us peace, and that peace is the foundation for all Christian living and victory.

We are now standing "in grace." Our salvation has not yet been completed, but "we rejoice in hope of the glory of God" (5:2). Hope points toward the future. First grace, then glory. Today we have a foretaste of the glory, but we rejoice in that day when Christ will appear and we shall be like Him. Meanwhile we have tribulation. We might expect the apostle to say that while we rejoice in the hope of that future glory, we are sad because of present tribulation. But here is one of the glorious paradoxes of the Gospel: "We also rejoice in our tribulations" (5:3). The reason is given for this rejoicing: "Tribulation" means the thing that presses down. It results in "endurance," literally, the thing that "holds up under"; this works out, or results in, "character," the passing of the test; "character produces hope," hope of the glory of God (5:4). God's great purpose is to mold us into the image of Christ, and the reason we can rejoice in tribulation is that this is one of the means by which we may grow from one degree of glory to another, in the likeness of Christ (2 Cor. 3:18). Thus, tribulation may be thought of as God's molding chisel, shaping us more and more into the likeness of Christ. This hope does not put to shame, as would a mere expectation of something in the future for which we have nothing to show in the present. We have an earnest of our inheritance. The assurance of being like Him in the future, is present likeness of Jesus. The love of God has been poured out abundantly in our hearts through the Holy Spirit, who is the earnest of our inheritance (5:5).

If that love of God led Him to give Christ for us when we were enemies, much more will that love be ours now that we are His friends. We will be saved from the future wrath of His judgment on sin, and not only that, but now in the present we shall be kept safe in the life of Jesus from the power of sin and judgment. And this love of God, shed abroad in our hearts, will reach out through us to others.

Observe how faith, hope and love are linked together here, and then notice the same glorious company in many other Scriptures (e.g., 1 Thess. 1:3; Col.1:4-1 Cor.13:13; Heb. 10:22-24).

4. CHRIST AND ADAM: GRACE AND RIGHTEOUSNESS CONTRASTED WITH LAW AND SIN—5:12-21

"Much more" is a key word of Romans 5. Contrasted with the wrath of judgment, condemnation and death resulting from sin are the "much mores" of God's exceeding grace. In this section "the first

Adam" and "the last Adam" are contrasted, "the first man" and "the second man from heaven." The key verse is: "where sin increased, grace abounded all the more" (5:20).

Man apart from Christ is contrasted with what man is in Christ, and the contrast is drawn by setting the one man Adam over against the one man Christ Jesus. Paul has brought Jew and Gentile together in Abraham, who is the father of all who have faith; now he brings all mankind together in Adam, the first man, through whom sin entered and passed on down through the race.

When Paul says, "So death spread to all men because all sinned" (5:12), obviously he is not speaking of the individual sins of each man. Many infants have died in infancy, and yet they did not sin personally. He means that when Adam sinned, he was the representative of the whole human race. In Adam all sinned, and all fell. However we may explain these things in theological terms, the fact is that all men are sinners, and that this sin began through the sin of our first parents. It was the woman, Eve, who sinned first, but it is the man who stands as the federal head of the race. Paul calls attention to the fact that "death reigned from Adam to Moses, even over those whose sinning was not like the transgression of Adam" (5:14), indicating that before the law was given through Moses, there was sin, and therefore, there was the breaking of God's law. Infants may be referred to as those who died, and yet did not sin as Adam did. Others would judge that Adam sinned by breaking a definite commandment of God, while those from Adam to Moses did not have the written law.

The central message in this passage is not the explanation of how sin came into the world, but it is the glorious message of salvation. Dr. A. J. Ramsey has said, "Romans 5 is God's hallelujah chorus, which man has turned into a funeral dirge…Beware of magnifying the shadow of Adam until it blots out the Light of the world." Paul does reveal the horror of sin. By the trespass of the one, the many died (vs. 15). That one trespass resulted in all of the anguish of the thousands of years of abounding sin. All men as a result were born sinners, and therefore, under God's condemnation, "Now the law came in to increase the trespass" (vs. 20). This does not mean that the law increased sin, but the law showed sin to be what it really is. One purpose was to awaken men to the meaning of this awful curse they were under (Gal. 3:24).

Against this background of abounding sin, Paul is declaring that "grace abounded all the more" (vs. 20). It was through the one man Adam that sin came. It was through the one man Christ Jesus that salvation came. In making this contrast, Paul is not saying that as all men are lost in Adam, so all men are saved in Christ. We know from the plain teaching of Scripture, and from the plain facts of human experience, that not all men are saved, and not all men are lost. The thought of Romans 5 is to show the relation between "the one" and "the many." Through the one man Adam, all the human race is under condemnation. Through the one man Christ, there is provided the free gift of salvation. This free gift does not merely offset what men lost in Adam. By the trespass of the one, death reigned. But those that receive the abundance of grace and of the gift of righteousness, reign in life through Jesus Christ in a way that is exceeding abundantly above all that was lost in Adam (vs. 17). The expression "those who receive the abundance of grace" indicates that there is a condition for entering into the provision of salvation through Christ. That condition is faith.

If it is quite clear that not all men are saved through the death of Christ, in what sense do all men who have partaken of the sin of Adam, partake also of the atonement of Christ? This presents us with the much-disputed question as to whether Christ died for all men, or only for the elect, those who will accept the Saviour and be saved. Some who believe in what is called "limited atonement" believe that the atonement that Christ made was made only for those whom God foreordained to be saved. Others, perhaps with more careful discrimination, have defined limited atonement as meaning that the application of Christ's atonement is limited to those who believe, and that in the purpose of God this, of course, was foreordained by Him. On the other side, there are teachers who believe that the atonement was equally for all men, and that God did not decree that the application of the atonement would be made to some and not to others.

As we face differences in interpretation of the Word, it is well to consider the points on which all interpreters agree. All agree that there is a universal offer of salvation by grace through faith. This offer is based on the atonement of Christ. Therefore, all agree that in some sense the atonement of Christ is for all men in the human race. The race is one; sin is one. Sin is against God, and God is one. The propitiation is made to God, and not to the devil, nor to man. The hindrance to God's forgiving sin was in the holy God, not in man. The good news that we can give to every sinner is: "Christ died for you."

The message of Romans 5 may be understood if we consider what state the human race would be in if Christ had not died. We are all children of Adam, born in sin. But there is the other side of the story, presented here in Romans 5. The history of the human race includes not only the first Adam, but the last Adam, not only the first man, but the second man from heaven. We are born into a race cursed with sin. But the glad news is that we have a Redeemer. And in the mystery of the grace of God the human race is to attain a height in Christ far greater than if sin had never been permitted to enter.

There is the sad, dark tragedy of those who reject the grace of God.

Yes, the tragedy is there. We cannot lightly eliminate it by teaching universal salvation, as some have attempted to do. Paul has clearly shown in the first section of Romans, "Sin Abounding," that all men who are lost are without excuse. In his section on "Grace Abounding for the Lost Sinner," he has brought the glad news that God has provided a righteousness which is a free gift, and is apart from any goodness in man. Now this presents a problem; but it is to be clearly noted that it is not a problem raised by the teaching of the Bible. It is a problem presented by the facts of sin, and the facts of salvation. God's Word reveals the truth. Man's experience confirms that truth of God's Word. What is the truth? The truth is that every man who is lost knows that he is lost by his own choice and through his own fault. He cannot put the blame on Satan, and he certainly cannot and will not put the blame on God. On the other hand, every man who is saved will ascribe all the glory, not some of it but all of it, to God alone. That is what grace means. He does not take to himself any credit. Faith excludes all boasting. Men do turn "faith" into a work, and boast of their faith. But down in our hearts we know that God has given us this faith, as He has provided everything in connection with salvation.

This truth is clear in the experience of Christians. Every Christian knows that he is responsible for every sin that he commits. His heart is grieved and he confesses the sin. But on the other hand, he does not take the glory to himself when by the grace of God he conquers sin. He says, "Every thought of holiness is His, and His alone." He knows that everything that comes short of the glory of God comes from himself, as everything that he does that is good the Holy Spirit is responsible for.

Much confusion has come about through the discussion of God's sovereignty and man's free agency by equating the two. But God's sovereignty is not to be considered parallel with man's free agency. God is the sovereign Creator. He created man with free will. Man sinned and lost his free will. He became a sinner. His will therefore is now in bondage. But he is still a free agent, responsible for his sin and responsible for turning to God. His nature now is sinful, and he will not turn to God apart from the grace of God. But men say, "If God has decreed that some will be saved, and decreed that others will be lost, how can man be responsible?" There is no place in the Bible which declares that God decreed that men should be lost. It is true that theologians speak of a "decree of reprobation," inferring that if God ordained some to be saved, then it follows logically that He has ordained others to be lost. But why should we go beyond Scripture in this? The fact is that all men in Adam are lost. God is dealing with a sinful human race, under the curse. He does not, therefore, need to decree that men shall be lost. They are lost. He does need to provide for salvation if any men are to be saved. This may seem a mere verbal distinction, but it goes deeper than that. God has provided a sufficient salvation. God by His grace has planned that a great multitude which no one can number will he saved through faith in Christ.

Scholars of all schools of thought believe that infants who die in infancy are saved through Christ's atonement. This does not mean that infants who die in infancy are innocent, and therefore do not need a Saviour. They need the atonement. But it seems quite clear that infants who are lost through no personal choice of their own are in the abounding grace of God saved apart from themselves, as they have not arrived at the age of accountability. Every infant that arrives at the age of accountability becomes a personal sinner, as they are a sinner even before they sin. To every individual who has become a personal sinner, there is the glad message of salvation through Christ. He or she must make a personal choice to receive Christ. There is no suggestion in

Scripture that anyone is lost except the one who has personally sinned.

"Sin reigned in death"—that is the sad story. But Christ died and rose again that "grace also might reign through righteousness leading to eternal life through Jesus Christ our Lord" (vs. 21).

Preparation for Lesson 5

Reading Lesson: Romans 6:1–7:6

Note: in this section we have three illustrations or pictures of what salvation means. "Are you ignorant?" Paul asks. Ignorant of what? Of what happened to us when we were saved.

A. *Dead to Sin and Alive to God* (6:1-14)

    1.   The first illustration is of *death and life*. Christians have died to sin. When did they? What does it mean to die to sin?

    2.   What does it mean to be united with Christ in His death and in His resurrection?

    3.   What is meant by the terms "old man" and "body of sin"? In what sense was our "old man" crucified and the "body of sin" destroyed?

    4.   Can you give a personal illustration of counting yourself dead unto sin?

    5.   In what way do we have defeat if we are "under law" and victory if we are "under grace"?

B. *Freed from the Old Master, Slaves of a New Master* (6:15-23)

    6.   The second illustration is that of *master and slave*. What is represented as the master before our salvation?

    7.   In what sense were we "made free from sin"? Does this mean we are sinless?

    8.   Do we as Christians have power to choose to obey our old master? What is our responsibility?

C. *Released from the Old Husband, Joined to the New* (7:1-6)

9. The third illustration is that of the *old husband and the new.* Who is represented by the wife whose husband dies and who marries another?

10. What fruit do we bring forth from our new union with Christ (Gal. 5:22-23)?

11. Three key words:

What three words indicate our responsibility in view of the truth of each of these three sections. The first word is "know." There is a fourth word that may be added. Mention each word with application to the passages.

Lesson 5

Grace Abounding for the Saint

Romans 6:1-8:39

The man who has been saved by grace through
faith is to go on living by grace through faith.

Key Verses: 6:4, 8:4, 8:37
"So we too might walk in newness of life" (6:4)
"Who walk not according to the flesh but according to the Spirit" (8:4)
"More than conquerors through him that loved us" (8:37)

God's plan of salvation by grace through faith is a revolutionary. Man in his natural reasoning knows nothing of the meaning of sin. So also he knows nothing of the meaning of God's righteousness, nor of the meaning of salvation as a free gift. Every natural instinct of a man's heart is to seek salvation by works, to merit heaven by his own goodness. This is true of the natural heart of both Jew and Gentile. The Jew turned God's revelation of grace into an excuse for seeking righteousness by works. Paul has cleared this all away by proving first that all men, Jews and Gentiles, are under sin, and that no man can do anything toward saving himself from sin. Then God provided a righteousness apart from anything that man can do. Man provided "sin abounding." God provided "grace abounding," by sending His own Son in the likeness of sinful flesh, and in that Son provided the complete obedience to every requirement of God's law for man, and the paying of the penalty for that broken law. Man's part is to believe. Such faith, of course, includes repentance for his sin, hatred of the sin and desire to turn from it. This repentance and faith is not a work that shows evidence of some merit in man. Grace means God giving. Faith means man receiving. It is not that faith constitutes a man's righteousness. The righteousness of Christ imputed to the man apart from anything in him is that which constitutes this perfect righteousness.

If I owe a debt of ten thousand dollars, with not one penny to pay it, and a friend out of his love should give me a check for ten thousand dollars, I would not pay any of that debt. It would be a free gift. He paid it all. I paid nothing. Such an illustration does not, of course, cover the whole truth with regard to sin. A money debt cannot picture the guilt of sin, and the debt against God because of my sin. However, it illustrates the one point that the righteousness of Christ is a free gift, and that faith is only the instrument by which that righteousness is received. There is the other truth that the Holy Spirit must enable a man, dead in trespasses and sin, to have the faith that receives the righteousness.

To the man who believes this revelation and accepts this astounding gift, there is peace in his heart; there is the joy of standing before God as though he had never sinned. There is the freedom that comes from having no condemnation.

But to the man who questions it, there arises a grave problem. It was the question his opponents put to Paul. It is the same question asked in many ways today. If this is truly the case of salvation, then can the man who accepts this redemption go right on sinning? There needs to be no change in his heart or his life. The righteousness is not his own. The righteousness is that of another, even Jesus Christ. This is a question that introduces the glorious section of Romans which we have designated "Grace Abounding for the Saint," or "Grace Abounding for the Saved Sinner."

1. UNDER GRACE A CHRISTIAN SHOULD NOT SIN; WHAT IS SALVATION? 6:1-7:6

"What shall we say then? Are we to continue in sin that grace may abound?" This is not a theoretical question, but one that was actually brought in objection to Paul's Gospel. The very fact that this question was raised indicates that Paul's Gospel is the good news of a perfect righteousness that is imputed to man apart from any works of his.

Paul rejects this conclusion not merely as a mistake, but as a complete misunderstanding of everything he has been saying. He exclaims, "Far from it!" or "May it never be," or "Never!" The strongest expression in English for indicating horror at some suggestion is the exclamation "God forbid!" Our English translators have used this, although in the original the word "God" does not appear, and perhaps would better not be used,

Paul in his answer to this question sets forth the whole glorious truth of God's plan for living a life of victory in Christ. However, he is not presenting a second salvation, or what is sometimes called a second work of grace. He sets forth first, what happens to a man when he is saved. He is not speaking here of something that God must do for a man after he is saved. He asks the question, "Are you ignorant?" Are you ignorant of what? It is not a matter of being ignorant of some deeper work of grace, nor of the baptism of the Spirit, nor of the fullness of the Spirit, nor of "entire sanctification." It is a matter of being ignorant of what happened to each Christian when he took Christ as his Saviour. To understand that is the basis for victorious living. Paul then proceeds to give three pictures to explain what salvation means. In doing this, he is answering the great theological question of the relation between justification and sanctification. Great theological problems arise because of great problems of experience. The right Scriptural answer to these problems gives the basis for a true experience.

A. SALVATION MEANS VITAL UNION WITH CHRIST, AND THAT MEANS SEPARATION FROM SIN—6:1-11

We Christians, Paul says, "died to sin." Paul goes on to show what this having died to sin means. It is something that is true of every Christian. The Christian may be ignorant of it, and as a result there may come defeat in his life. It is something that we ought to know— that we who are baptized into Christ Jesus are baptized into His death and into His resurrection. Salvation means union with Christ. The justification that Paul has been speaking about in Romans 3:21–5:21, is accompanied by the great miracle of union with Christ by the power of the Holy Spirit. Salvation means union with Christ. We are not justified on the ground of our union with Christ. We are declared righteous on the ground of Christ's righteousness, which is set down to our account. But when we take Christ as our Saviour, we are born of the Spirit, and we are baptized by the Spirit into the Body of Christ. We are united with Him. Paul in this chapter is not discussing water baptism. It is important to be baptized with water, because the Lord has commanded it. But this water baptism is an outward symbol of the great miracle of the baptism of the Holy Spirit which joins us to Christ.

What does this union with Christ mean? It does not mean sinlessness. It does not mean the completion of our salvation. Paul explains that this is union with Christ in His death and in His resurrection. All that the death of Christ meant, it meant for us. Christ died to sin, once for all, and in Christ we died. But Christ was raised from the dead. We are united with Him in that resurrection. As a result, we Christians walk in newness of life. We have a new life.

Paul says that our old man was crucified with Christ. This is the same truth as expressed in Galatians 2:20: "I have been crucified with Christ." Our "old man" is all that we were in Adam. The expression "old man" is set in contrast with the "new man." It is used in two other places. In Colossians 3:9 it is said, "Do not lie to one another, seeing that you have put off the old self with its practices." These expressions are used in the sense of a contrast. The new came when the old went. In Ephesians 4:22 we are exhorted to "to put off your old self, which belongs to your former manner of life...and to put on the new self." Some would interpret this to mean that each Christian has put away the old man. In any case, the emphasis here is that we are to cease living after the manner of the old man. It does not mean that we are progressively to put away something within us called "the old man," but that we are to put the "old man" away "as concerning your former manner of life." One of the doings of the old man is lying. Christians are not to lie to one another. This does not mean that Christians cannot lie. The sad truth is that Christians do lie and thus grieve the Spirit of truth.

Paul says that our old man was crucified with Christ, "that the body of sin might be brought to nothing." This "body of sin" does not mean some totality of sin, or some special entity within us which is called "the body of sin." The word "body" is always used by Paul as referring to the human body, either literally or in a figurative or spiritual way. "The body of sin" therefore, refers to this body, either as the instrument of sin, or as the slave of sin, that is, under the control of sin. The expression "brought to nothing" does not mean "destroyed," but "rendered inoperative" as some translate it. The same word is used in

Romans 7:6, and translated "discharged." The practical message is that this body that was used for sin, might be discharged from its business of sinning. This is made clear in the last phrase of verse 6, "that we would no longer be enslaved to sin."

The glad truth of this paragraph is that we who have become united with Christ in the likeness of His death are also united in the likeness of His resurrection. We are joined to the risen Christ. The practical conclusion is: "Even so, reckon also yourselves to be dead to sin, but alive to God in Christ Jesus." This word "reckon" means "to count on the fact." Some seem to use it in the sense of "make believe that you are dead to sin." Others judge that the reckoning ourselves to be dead unto sin gives us victory over sin. But this glorious statement of Paul's is not connected with our subjective feeling, nor with a state of being "dead to sin," which comes as a result of our reckoning. He explains the sense in which every Christian is "dead to sin." He is exhorting us to reckon that thing to be true. The reckoning does not make it true. It is true. We are therefore to reckon upon it.

Much confusion has resulted from a wrong conception of what it means to be "dead to sin." It is told of one the Church fathers that a student asked him what it meant to be "dead to sin." The teacher took him to the grave of Chrysostom, the famous golden-tongued preacher of the fourth century, honored for his great sanctity. The father told the pupil to express to Chrysostom his admiration for him. The young man told of all the wonderful things that Chrysostom had done. "What effect does it have on him?" the father asked. "Father, he is dead; it has no effect upon him." Then the father asked the young man to criticize the dead preacher, and heap accusations against him. Again there was no effect. "Now you know what it means to be dead to sin."

This, of course is exactly what it does not mean. If we were in a place where temptation did not appeal to us, and where we would be as senseless as the dead body of Chrysostom was to praise or blame, there would be no need to tell us to reckon ourselves dead unto sin. The plain meaning is that we are to count on the fact that we belong to Christ, and that we are separated from sin. The result of that would, of course, be that we will hate sin and seek in every way to "live to God."

The illustration of this truth often given in the New Testament is in the marriage relationship. The man who is married reckons on the fact that he is joined to one woman, and by that fact is separated from all other women in that relationship.

B. FREED FROM THE OLD MASTER, SLAVES OF THE NEW— 6:12-23

The second picture Paul gives to explain what happens when we are saved is the picture of slavery and freedom. In summing up the message of the first paragraph, he exhorts Christians not to let sin reign or be king "in your mortal body," that is, in this body, "to make you obey its passions." This refers to the desires of the body. To obey those desires and thus to act contrary to the will of God is to let sin reign. Sin is here personified. He is not speaking of sin as some entity dwelling within a Christian, though it is certainly true in the spiritual reality that sin is in the Christian. He says, "Do not present your members to sin as instruments for unrighteousness, but present yourselves to God as those who have been brought from death to life, and your members to God as instruments for righteousness." We have died and have risen, and we are now walking in newness of life. The logic of that position is then to act as those alive from the dead, and yield our bodies and all our desires to God for His control, "For sin will have no dominion over you, since you are not under law."

If we were "under law," sin would have dominion over us. What does this mean? For one thing, if we were "under law," we would be subject to the penalty of the law, because we have broken it. And the wages of sin is death. We, however, are not under condemnation. The law has lost all of its terror. We have the righteousness of Christ. If we were "under law," we would not only be subject to the death penalty for the broken law, but we would be under obligation to keep the law perfectly every moment of our lives, as the ground of our righteousness. The glad news is that we are "under grace." If we were under law, everything would depend on our power to keep the law, and on our power to make atonement for the broken law. But "under grace," everything depends on the power of Christ. He paid the penalty. We are joined to Him, and He gives power to live in newness of life. This expression "under law," as we shall see in later passages, does not mean that the moral law of God is not a standard nor a rule for Christian living; for in that sense law is simply an expression of the will of God. Christ delighted to do His will: "Your law is within my heart." Grace does not mean that a man is excused from doing the will of God, but grace is God's marvelous provision for enabling a man to do His will.

But again the question is raised: "Shall we sin because we are not under the law, but under grace?" Again he rejects the suggestion with horror, and explains what happened to us when we were saved: that we were delivered, or set free completely, from the bondage of our old master sin, and that we were bought with a price, and became slaves of a new Master. Again Paul is using a figure of speech, the figure of personification. He contrasts being slaves of sin, personified as a master, or slaves of obedience, personified as a master. In the one case to be a slave of sin means death. In the other case, to be a slave of obedience means righteousness. He gives thanks that where they were once the slaves of sin, they became obedient to the Gospel and were set free from sin (vs. 17.18). This does not mean they were made sinless. As a slave is set free from the old master, and becomes a slave of the new master, so we are set free from sin as a master and became a slave of the Lord Jesus Christ. It is clear that this truth, whatever its meaning, applies to all Christians, and not to a particular group who are surrendered or victorious or more intelligent than other Christians. Every Christian has been set free from sin, in the sense in which the Holy Spirit is using those words. We ought not to give the words a meaning different from that which Paul, speaking in the Spirit, intends.

We have been set free from sin in the sense that the eternal death penalty of sin has been paid. The penalty of the broken law cannot in any degree be laid upon the one who is in Christ Jesus. He has the righteousness of Christ. But we are also set free from sin in the sense that we do not need to obey our old master. We are now slaves of righteousness, which means that we are slaves of the Lord Jesus Christ. Christ has set us free from both the penalty of sin and the power of sin.

In presenting God's plan of salvation, we often use Romans 3:23 "All have sinned," and link it with Romans 6:23, "For the wages of sin is death: but the free gift of God is eternal life in Christ Jesus our Lord." This verse shows that he is still speaking of salvation by grace through faith, and the relation of this to our daily living.

C. FROM THE OLD HUSBAND, TO THE NEW—7:1-6

Paul patiently recognizes that his readers may still be ignorant of this great message of freedom. He therefore uses another illustration, the picture of the marriage relationship, to bring out the same truth of freedom from the curse of the law and the bondage of sin. They are all acquainted with the law of matrimony. The woman is bound by law to the husband while he lives: "but if her husband dies she is released from the law of marriage" (7:2). This does not mean that the law of matrimony is done away. It means that she is discharged from that law. While she is married, she is under that law. If she should marry another man, she has broken the law, and is an adulteress.[1]

As this woman was joined to her old husband by the law of matrimony, Paul writes, so we were once joined to sin, and the law held us in its grip. The fruit of that marriage was death. But as Christians we "have died to the law through the body of Christ." The former husband has died, just as our old man was crucified with Christ. Christ was made sin for us, died and was raised from the dead. Now we are joined to Him, the living Christ, and from that union we are to bring forth fruit for God.

Many have been the discussions as to who the old husband is. Many are the discussions also as to what it means to be "discharged from the law." The central truth is the same as that in the sixth chapter. He is speaking of our identification with Christ. Christ died and rose again. Christ paid the penalty of the law. Christ died unto sin, and now lives unto God. We are joined with Christ. The law no longer has any hold upon us. If it did have a hold upon us, we would be under the curse of the law, and we would be under the bondage of sin. Before she could be joined to a new husband, the woman's first husband must die. Before we can live in newness of life, we must be clear forever from the penalty of the broken law, and from the bondage of having to keep the letter of the law as a means of righteousness.

---

1 We should note here that Paul is not discussing whether or not there is Scriptural ground for divorce. How unfitting it would be when he is using marriage as an illustration of freedom from the law, to refer to the case of a woman who is divorced from her husband because of unfaithfulness.

Paul sums it up in verses 5 and 6. Before we were saved we were "in the flesh." We were under the law. The passions of sin wrought in our members. The result was death—spiritual death in the present, and eternal, unending death unless deliverance should come. Then follows another glorious "but." "But *now* we are released from the law." We are no longer under its curse. We are no longer under its obligation as a means of righteousness. We have died to that wherein we were held. How did we die? Christ died for us, and rose again. We are united with Christ, identified with Him in His death and resurrection.

This great deliverance works out actually in our lives. Was the sin of the old life real? When we were in the flesh, did the passions of sin have a real effect? Just as real is the new life, when passion for Christ controls and we serve in newness of spirit. Our English translations have a small letter for "spirit," indicating that the contrast is between the outward letter of the law and the inward spirit. Of course, it is by the power of the Holy Spirit, as he later explains, that we serve in the newness of spirit. The thought here, however, is the contrast between trying to keep the outward letter of the law and rejoicing in serving a Saviour whom we love. It is the contrast between the burden of trying to be good and the delight of serving Christ.

D. OUR RESPONSIBILITY IN VIEW OF GOD'S GRACE

We have seen in this sixth chapter of Romans a declaration of what God has done for every believer. Only confusion results when we read this section as an exhortation to Christians to produce in their experience a deliverance and freedom that is spoken of. This passage is the good news of God's provision. It is not stating what God will do. It is a declaration of what God has done. What then is the responsibility of the Christian?

There are three words in Romans 6 that make clear our responsibility. The first is the word "know." The question is asked, "do you not know?" or "Are you ignorant?" The clear implication is that Christians may be ignorant of this good news of their identification with Christ in His death and resurrection. Such ignorance will certainly lead to defeat. Therefore, our responsibility is to know the good news of God's plan for living the Christian life by the supernatural power of the Spirit, under grace.

The second word, using the order in Romans, is the word "reckon." We are to count upon these truths that God has declared. Here again it is possible for a Christian not to reckon on this fact of his union with Christ and the indwelling of the Holy Spirit.

The third word is "yield." We surrender our very selves to Christ, not in order to produce this new resurrection life. We are to yield as alive from the dead, or because we are alive from the dead.

We may think of the yielding as coming first in the order of thought or in the application to our own experience. There are Christians who are fully yielded to Christ so far as their desire to have Him control every action, and yet are defeated. The reason is that they have not believed the good news that they are joined to Christ and that Christ is meeting every need.

There is a fourth word that may be added which suggests the secret of continuance in victory. This is the word "obey" which may be thought of as "abide." Dr. Griffith Thomas has spoken of the *crisis,* followed by the *process.* Having adopted as our life attitude that we have yielded to Christ and are trusting Him, we have God's provision in what the theologians have called "the means of grace." If we are to abide in Christ, we need to feed on the Word, give ourselves to prayer, worship regularly in the church services, partake of the Lord's supper, have fellowship with other Christians, witness for Christ, grow in grace and in the knowledge of Christ. All of these things are essential as we go on in the Christian life, and they are God's provision, the means by which we abide.

Preparation for Lesson 6

Reading Lesson: Romans 6–8

The Struggle of Romans 7 (7:7-25)

1. Does this passage describe a personal experience of Paul? If so, when did he have it? Does every Christian have this experience? Is it the experience of a saved or an unsaved man?

2. In what sense have you had an experience like this before you were saved? After you were saved?

3. Read carefully Romans 7:5-6. What contrast is drawn in these two verses between what Christians once were, in the past, and what they are now, in the present? Does this give light on the subject of 7:7-25?

4. What does Paul say is the character of the law of God? Why has it this character? What is the purpose of the law?

5. How does the law convict us of sin? What is the present relation of the law and the Christian?

6. What causes the struggle and defeat as revealed in this passage? What is shown as the way of deliverance from it? When does this deliverance come?

Lesson 6

The Struggle of Romans Seven

Romans 7:7-25

Having come thus far in the glorious message of deliverance through Christ, we must face the burning question as to the place that sin has in the daily living of Christians. If serving "in newness of the spirit" means that a Christian is sinless, there is no particular problem. But we know from experience, as well as from God's revelation, that it does not mean this. Our salvation is not yet complete. The practical question arises then as to whether all Christians are sinning, and if the difference among Christians is a difference only in degree. If so, what is the difference between a Christian's sinning and an unsaved man's sinning? These questions are dealt with in the seventh chapter of Romans, and great has been the contest among interpreters as to what Paul is really saying in this passage. Before studying the text, we may find it helpful to consider as a background some of the main interpretations that have been given:

Paul is describing his own personal experience as a Jew before he was saved, trying to keep the law.

Paul is describing his experience after he was saved, but before he learned the secret of deliverance.

Paul is describing the experience of seeking righteousness by keeping the law. This might apply to an unsaved man who accepts God's standard, like the pious Jew, or to a Christian who has not been enlightened as to God's way of living by the power of the Spirit.

Paul is describing the struggle between the old nature and the new nature, a struggle which takes place in every Christian. He explains the way of deliverance in this struggle.

Paul is describing the normal experience of every Christian in his struggle with sin.

Paul is describing the struggle and defeat of Christians who have not been entirely sanctified, or who have not received the second work of grace, or the baptism of the Holy Spirit.

When equally devoted and equally learned interpreters differ so radically on a passage of Scripture, it usually means that there may be truth in the various views, and that the truth is not to be found by insisting too dogmatically on a strong emphasis on one phase of the truth to the ignoring or denying of other phases of the truth.

We need not be concerned to fit this teaching into any particular phase of Paul's own experience. If he were giving a personal testimony, it would not necessarily have any authority for other Christians. We have here the teaching of the Holy Spirit given through Paul. The fact that he uses the personal pronoun "I" does not mean that he is giving a personal testimony, except as it applies universally.

In a somewhat parallel case, Paul writes: "But if through my lie God's truth abounds to his glory, why am I still being condemned as a sinner?" (3:7). No one would suppose that he personally had told this lie. It is a vivid way of setting forth the truth. And so we may regard it in Romans 7. This does not mean that in his own experience Paul did not have this experience mentioned in the seventh chapter of Romans, but he had it only as every human being in his circumstances also has it.

He begins by asking one of those questions which evidently were actually asked by his opponents: "Is the law sin?" The Jews accused Paul of talking against the law. He has said that Christians were discharged from the law. That might sound as though the law were a bad thing, something that we needed to be delivered from. He spurns such a suggestion. He goes on to explain one of the great purposes of the law. He would not have known what sin was except through the law. Then he gives an illustration from one of the ten commandments. He would not have known coveting, that is, he would not have been convicted of the sin of coveting, unless the law had said, "You shall not covet."

It is striking that Paul passes over nine of the commandments and chooses the tenth. Paul might have gone through all of these nine commandments and given himself a perfect score on every one, so far as the outward keeping of the law is concerned. But the tenth commandment had to do with inward desire. It is not true that Paul, nor any other Jew, had kept the other nine commandments. In the Sermon on the Mount our Lord reveals the inner meaning of those commandments. A man might keep the commandment "You shall not murder" so far as actually murdering another is concerned. But the true keeping of that commandment is to love our neighbors as ourselves. Whoever is angry with his brother in his heart has broken that commandment. A man may not be a thief in the eyes of the law. But if he does not love his neighbor and guard his neighbor's property as he would his own, then he has broken the eighth commandment. Paul never broke the command "You shall not commit adultery." The Jews in general lived on a high plane so far as outward immorality was concerned, compared with other nations. But our Lord indicated that if a man looked on a woman to lust after her, he had broken that commandment. The word "lust" is the same word that means "desire," whether that desire is good or evil. Impurity in the inner desire is sin. This does not mean, of course, that it is just as bad to desire something in the heart as to commit the outward act. When murder or adultery is committed, that is the inward desire carried to its final culmination. The tenth commandment, therefore, suggests the inner meaning of all commandments. The requirement of the law is to love God with our whole being, and to love our neighbors as ourselves. A man considers that he has not sinned, according to his own standard; but when he faces the holy commandment of God he is convicted of sin. And so Paul says that through the commandment he was convicted of "all manner of coveting."

Paul says, "I was once alive apart from the law." Whether this means before a man comes to the age of accountability, or before he becomes acquainted with God's law, or before he has a conviction of his sin, the truth is clear. One of the purposes of God's law is to convict a man of his sin. The commandment was intended to be unto life. If a man should keep these commandments to love God supremely, and to love his neighbor as himself, the result would be real life. But since he has not done it, and cannot do it, the commandment has become death to him.

Paul now answers the question as to whether the law is sin. No, "the law is holy, and the commandment is holy and righteous and good" (vs. 12). How then could a holy, righteous thing become death to me? It was not the law that brought the death. It was my breaking of the law. It was sin. The law, with its death penalty, was to reveal sin, in order that it might be shown to be what it is.

Paul then goes on from verse 14 to give that vivid description of the great struggle. It has been described as the struggle of a man face to face with law, knowing that the law is good, striving to keep it and being wretched because he cannot do it. Is this man a normal Christian, or a defeated Christian, or one who has never been born again?

One writer has stated: "Romans 7:14-24 is not a Christian experience. With the exception of the revelation of the law as spiritual, there is not a single Christian word, or thought, or expression, in the whole passage. There is no mention of Christ. There is no mention of the Holy Spirit. Every word could have been written if Christ had never come to the earth. There is failure and defeat at every step, a struggle that ends in wretchedness. Can this be Christian? It is not a Christian experience, but it may be the experience of a Christian."

On the other hand, there is the interpretation that this struggle describes the experience of every born-again child of God. It is held that it cannot refer to an unsaved man because of the statement, "For I delight in the law of God, in my inner being" (vs. 22). Dr. A. J. Ramsey has suggested that if Romans 7 describes the normal Christian experience we must change our Lord's invitation to read: "Come to me all who labor and are heavy laden, and I will tell you how to be wretched, by presenting the requirements of the law and revealing that you cannot keep them!"

"If this is Paul's personal experience," we ask, "how can it fit with Paul's statement in the beginning of Romans, 'Paul, a slave of Jesus Christ,' and with his cry of triumph, 'But thanks be to God, who in Christ always leads us in triumphal procession' (2 Cor. 2:14) or with his other word, 'I can do all things through him who strengthens me.' (Phil. 4:13)." All of the other testimonies Paul gives appear to be testimonies of triumph. He calls on other Christians to imitate him: "What you have learned and received and heard and seen in me—practice these things, and the God of peace will be with you" (Phil. 4:9).

As we interpret Romans 7, we must take account of the undoubted fact that a multitude of Christians have testified that this was exactly their experience before they took Christ as Saviour. A drunkard struggling with his addiction might well read this paragraph line by line as an expression of his experience. Thousands of earnest, orthodox Jews in Russia, and other lands, have been striving for centuries to keep the commandments of God, and have cried out in defeat and despair, "Wretched man that I am!" It is a questionable thing to interpret this passage in such a way as to say that no unsaved man can have this experience. The word, "For I delight in the law of God, in my inner being," means that with the mind I approve the law of God. Many a man does that before he is saved. Many a man, convicted by the Holy Spirit, can say, "For I have the desire to do what is right, but not the ability to carry it out" (vs. 18).

On the other hand, it is just as certain that there are born-again Christians who know what this struggle means. Indeed, can we say that there is any Christian who has not had this experience?

Let us notice first some wrong conclusions that may be drawn from this chapter. This will help us to arrive at the central truth.

Suppose I should say that this struggle applies only to unsaved people? When I take Christ as my Saviour, such a struggle ceases. If this were true, then no one who sins is a Christian. There has been a teaching that when a person is born again, he becomes sinless, and that whenever sin enters, he ceases to be Christian. This view is obviously wrong.

Some view the struggle as the experience of every Christian who has not had a second work of grace. Suppose I judge that there is a second crisis, and that in this crisis I have been "entirely sanctified"? Then the struggle ceases. That ought to mean that an entirely sanctified person cannot sin, and if he does sin, he ceases not only to be sanctified, but he ceases to be saved. In any case, there is no suggestion of two kinds of Christians here, or of a first work of grace and a second work of grace.

Another view is that of a dualism, namely, that a Christian has an entity called "sin" dwelling within him, and that this sin or sin-nature is in conflict with a new nature that he receives at regeneration. But there is no evidence in this description that Paul is talking about two contrary natures. It is the man himself who has the struggle. When he says, "So now it is no longer I who do it, but sin that dwells within me" (vs. 17), he does not mean that he is not responsible for the sin. He means that he has no more control over his own actions. He does not want to sin. It is he that is doing the sin, but he recognizes that he has a master. Sin is spoken of here as the master who lives in him and controls the house.

Suppose, then, I judge that this is a description of the normal Christian experience? It surely gives the impression of defeat, and also discouragement, because the man cries out, "Wretched man that I am!" It is to be feared that a large number of Christians take some comfort in the fact that this paragraph describes them, and therefore they have the evidence that they are Christians. Surely there is something wrong with this interpretation. The chapter should not be a comfort to those who continue to live defeated Christian lives, but a challenge to a life of victory by the power of the Holy Spirit.

When this man cries out, "Wretched man that I am! Who shall deliver me out of the body of this death?" there is an answer to his cry. It is a triumphant answer. He cries, "Thanks be to God through Jesus

Christ our Lord!" (vs. 25).

Then he sums up the argument, "So then I of myself with the mind, indeed, serve the law of God; but with the flesh the law of sin" (vs. 25). Two main interpretations have been given to this: "I, left to myself, apart from the power of the Holy Spirit, can do only one thing: with the mind I can approve the law of God and in that sense serve the law; but with the flesh, in the actual practise of my life, I serve the law of sin." The other translation of the verse is: "So then, I myself serve the law of God with my mind, but with my flesh I serve the law of sin." This interpretation seems to close on a negative note of failure. The same person goes on approving the law of God with the mind, but breaking that law in actual practice. This does not fittingly introduce the message of Romans 8: "There is therefore now no condemnation for those who are in Christ Jesus."

If we interpret Romans 7 aright, we will on the one hand agree that Christians are not sinless. Our redemption is not complete. We are living in a body that makes us, of ourselves, capable of nothing but sin. Every Christian can say, "For I know that nothing good dwells in me, For I have the desire to do what is right, but not the ability to carry it out" (vs. 18). Every Christian recognizes that any good that is in him is there by the grace of God and by the power of the Holy Spirit: "Every thought of holiness is His, and His alone."

If that were the end of the story, then the Christian indeed would be wretched. But that is not the end of the story. Paul goes on in chapter 8 to explain the wonderful working of God the Holy Spirit in every believer. He will explain that our bodies are dead because of sin, incapable of righteousness. But we have the earnest of our inheritance; we have the Holy Spirit. Paul says, "For I know that nothing good dwells in me, that is, in my flesh"; but Paul also says, "I can do all things through Christ who strengthens me." No Christian has in himself the power to do that which is good. If the indwelling of the Holy Spirit in the Christian meant that all sin were cast out, and that the man were sinless, there would be no conflict of this kind. But that is not the case. When we have a resurrection body like the body of our Lord, this will be the situation. Meanwhile, there is sin dwelling in us. But we have already heard the good news that sin shall not have dominion over us.

What, then, is the practical secret of victory revealed in the seventh chapter of Romans? First there is the conviction of the need: "O wretched man that I am!" A vision of the holiness of God and the righteous requirements of His law is bound to bring to me a conviction of my own failure in sin. Anything that falls short of supreme love to God is sin. The closer a Christian lives to the Lord, the more poignant is his anguish in the knowledge that he has said or thought or done something to grieve the Spirit. He has spoken something that is not absolute truth. He has thought something that has been a thought of pride and self. He has looked with unchaste desire. He has failed to do something which love prompted him to do. Is he to be miserable because he does not have the power to do that which is good? Surely these very failures are calling him to the secret of victory by grace through faith.

Dr. C. I. Scofield was preaching on the seventh chapter of Romans and saying that a Christian should come out of the place of struggle and defeat of the seventh chapter of Romans into the eighth of Romans, the place of victory by the power of the Spirit. A well-dressed gentleman came to him at the close of the service and said, "Doctor, I don't see why Paul had such a hard time being good. I don't find it hard to be good."

"What do you mean by being good?"

"Oh, what everybody means—living a clean moral life, being

honest, paying your debts; if your neighbor gets in trouble, put your hand in your pocket and help him out."

"Paul did those things all his life. Any gentleman would do that. You do not need to be a Christian to live that way. That is not what Paul meant by being good."

"Well, what in the world did he mean?"

"Did you ever try to be meek?" the minister asked.

"What's that?"

"Did you ever try to be meek?"

"No, sir! I don't admire a meek man."

"Well, God does. His Son was meek and lowly. But suppose some day you started out to determine that you were going to be meek, that you were going to love everyone that you were going to meet every situation with love and kindness. Would you find it easy?"

"No, sir! That's not in my line! I'm not built that way!"

Just so. We are not built that way. That business man, probably a church member, was very far from the meaning of victory through the power of the Lord. He needed the message of the seventh chapter of Romans. He needed to cry out, "O wretched man that I am!"

One night a little five-year-old daughter of a friend of mine climbed onto her father's knee when he came home in the evening and said, "Daddy, did you notice that I bowed my head and shut my eyes? Daddy, I was a naughty girl today."

"Were you, Annie?"

"Yes, Daddy. And do you know, Daddy, now whenever I am naughty, I bow my head and shut my eyes and ask Jesus to forgive me."

"And He does, doesn't He, dear?"

"Yes, Daddy."

Then the little girl seemed to be very thoughtful, and after some moments of silence she burst out with the problem of her heart: "Daddy, it's awful hard to be good, isn't it?"

This little girl, five years old, was beginning to understand something of the message of Romans 7, which the strong-minded business man had missed. That message is that it is utterly impossible for any human being to be good apart from the enabling grace of the Holy Spirit, and it is utterly impossible for any Christian to be sinlessly perfect in this life. Since that is so, shall we accept the standard of most Christians and live in defeat, and failure, and struggle, and declare that this is the normal Christian experience?

A minister friend of mine had a brother-in-law who was a physician. This brother-in-law said to him one day, when the minister was speaking to him about the secret of victory:

"You see, I'm like Paul."

"Hold on a minute," his brother said. "I confess I never had noticed the resemblance before. And I want to remind you that you are paying yourself no small compliment to say that you are like Paul."

Before his brother-in-law recovered from this new approach to the subject, he added: "Also, I want to warn you not to slander a man in his absence."

What this physician meant was what many Christians mean when they say, "I am like Paul." They mean that the good that they would, they do not, and the evil that they would not, that they practice. But this is the story of Paul, apart from the enabling grace of the Lord.

The first step in the victory is the consciousness of the need. The next step is revealed in that word, "Who will deliver me?" Not, why does the Lord permit us to have this struggle? Not, when will I get rid of this struggle? Not, how am I to have the victory? Not, what is the right doctrine about holiness? But it is who? Since there is Someone to bring deliverance, my part surely is to surrender my life to the control of that One. The next step in victory is to say: "Thanks be to God through Jesus Christ our Lord!" That is faith. That is walking by the Spirit.

It is not, therefore, wrong to say that the struggle described in the seventh chapter of Romans is the experience of the Christian. But the thing that is wrong is the emphasis that is placed on the negative message of sin and defeat. For the Christian, this is the background for the cry of victory. Paul goes on in the eighth chapter of Romans to describe this plan of grace abounding for the Christian. However, we are not to think of the sixth chapter of Romans and the eighth chapter of Romans as giving a message of salvation by grace through faith, and the seventh chapter of Romans as describing something that leaves out the message of Victory. Some interpret it that way. They take it as a parenthesis to indicate what happens if the man tries to be good under the law. It is true that if a man struggles and strives to keep the law in his own strength the result will be wretchedness. But there is another truth, namely, that this Christian who has been united to Christ by the power of the Holy Spirit is not yet made perfect. He must take account of the fact that his body has not yet been redeemed and that he himself is not sinless. Sin is there. This truth the seventh chapter of Romans makes clear, but not in order to leave a man in wretchedness, because the response to the question "Who will deliver?" is in the seventh chapter, before we come to the eighth: "Thanks be to God through Jesus Christ our Lord!"

Preparation for Lesson 7

Flesh Way and Spirit Way contrasted (8:1-14)

1. Someone has suggested that each of the first four verses of Romans 8 sums up the message of a chapter of Romans. Can you tell to which chapter each verse applies?

2. Put on one side all that these verses say about "walking after the flesh" and on the other all that is said concerning "walking after the Spirit." What is the personal application of the message?

3. What is meant by "the mind of the flesh"? By "the doings of the body"?

4. To what does giving life to our mortal bodies refer? (See 8:11.)

5. What would you say is the secret of victory over sin revealed in these verses?

6. What contrasts do you notice between Romans 7 and 8?

7. Count the times the word "I" occurs in Romans 7 and in Romans 8 and the number of times the word "Spirit" occurs in chapter 7 and chapter 8.

Lesson 7

Threefold Salvation of the Christian

Romans 8:1-14

3. DEBTORS NOW TO WALK AFTER THE SPIRIT, NOT AFTER THE FLESH—8:1–8:13

"The greatest chapter in the Bible" is the way many have expressed their view of Romans 8. It is pre-eminently the chapter of the Holy Spirit, because the truth concerning the Holy Spirit in the life of a Christian is set forth in this chapter more fully than in any other chapter in the Bible. It is striking that in Romans 7:7-25 the word "I" occurs thirty-one times (in the English version), and the Holy Spirit is not mentioned once. In Romans 8 the Holy Spirit is directly mentioned seventeen times; the word "I" occurs twice, "I consider" (vs. 18) and "I am sure" (vs. 38). Two good ways to use "I".

The threefold salvation of the Christian is set forth in this chapter. We have been saved by grace—*salvation begun* (Eph. 2:8). We are kept by the power of God, and His grace is sufficient—*salvation present*, or salvation continued (1 Pet. 1:5; 2 Cor. 12:9). We look forward to that grace that is to be brought to us at the revelation of Jesus Christ— *salvation future*, or salvation completed (1 Pet. 1:13).

When a Christian takes Christ as Saviour, he is born of the Spirit (John 3:5, 8); he has the witness of the Spirit (Rom. 8:16); is baptized by the Spirit into the Body of Christ (1 Cor. 12:13); he is indwelt by the Spirit (Rom. 8:9; 1 Cor. 3:16, 6:19).

The one who is born of the Spirit is to walk by the Spirit (Gal. 5:25);
be led by the Spirit (Rom. 8:14): be filled with the Spirit (Eph. 5:18);
bear the fruit of the Spirit (Gal. 5:22-23). This is grace abounding for
present living. But we are saved "in hope." When we take Christ as our
Saviour, we are sealed with the Spirit unto the day of redemption (Eph.
4:30). We have the earnest of the Spirit, a foretaste of the complete
inheritance (Eph. 1:14). We have the first-fruits of the Spirit, which
look forward to the completed harvest, in us individually and in the
whole Body of Christ (Rom. 8:23).

These glorious facts about our "so great salvation" are set forth in
a wonderful way in Romans 8. Usually we speak of this as salvation
past, present, future. Perhaps we could better describe this as salvation
begun, salvation continued, salvation completed.

Dr. Griffith Thomas has suggested that the first four verses of
Romans 8 sum up the message of chapters 5 to 8: (1) no condemnation—chapter 5; (2) set free from the law of sin and death—chapter
6; (3) what the law could not do—chapter 7; (4) walking not after the
flesh, but after the Spirit—chapter 8.

One of the key expressions of chapter 8 is "in Christ." First there
is that great theme of justification by faith, no condemnation to those
who are in Christ. His perfect righteousness is ours. He links this
immediately with the work of the Holy Spirit: "the law of the Spirit of
life"; this refers to the Holy Spirit. When we were in the flesh we were
not only under condemnation, but we were in bondage to the law of
sin and death. Now in Christ we have been set free. What the law could
not do, God did. Paul has shown that the law is holy and spiritual. But
the law could not make a dead man live. Because we are sinful, we are
not able to keep the law. But there came One in the, likeness of the
flesh of sin: truly man, though apart from sin, and He condemned sin

in the flesh. He won the victory. He paid the penalty, and He kept the law perfectly. He did all this for us.

There is a dispute as to whether Christ coming "for sin" refers to His atonement, coming as "an offering for sin," or "on the business of sin." In any case, the emphasis here is the deliverance that Christ gives from the power of sin. The purpose of all of this is that the righteous requirement of God's law might be fulfilled in us. Some interpret this as referring to the righteousness of Christ which is imputed to us. But the teaching here evidently is concerned with the daily living of Christians who have been set free not only from the penalty but also from the power of sin. We might paraphrase: "That the righteous requirement of God's law might be fulfilled in us as we keep walking not after the flesh, but after the Spirit." The following verses describe these two ways of walking, or living.

They who are walking after the flesh are they who are minding or giving attention to the things of the flesh: they that are "after the Spirit" are they who are minding the things of the Spirit: "for the minding of the flesh is death; but the minding of the Spirit is life and peace."

The word translated "mind" in our English version is not a noun, but a verbal noun, that is, a noun that expresses the result of the action of the verb from which it is formed. In Ephesians 2:10, "We are his workmanship," we have such a verbal noun, meaning that we are the result of His working. In the same way the word translated "mind of the flesh" (unfortunately translated "carnal mind" in the old version) means the result of minding the things of the flesh.

The expressions "the flesh," "the mortal body," "the body of sin," "the desire of the body," "the body is dead," "the deeds of the body" are used by Paul in contrast to such expressions as: "the Spirit," "the inward man," "members as instruments of righteousness," "minding of the

Spirit," "life through your mortal body," "the spirit is life." The former are on the side of sin and death, the latter on the side of life and righteousness. They are all used primarily with a spiritual, not a physical, significance; for example, we are told to "put to death the doings of the body"; when we let our bodily appetites control, and thus walk after the flesh, our actions are referred to as "the doings of the body." All the good things that we do might be spoken of as "doings of the body." But here the word "body" is used as the seat of sin, and this expression would be equivalent to the "works of the flesh."

Thus Paul in Romans 8 is speaking of two ways of living which are entirely opposite. The minding of the flesh is enmity against God. They that are "in the flesh" cannot please God. Those "in the flesh" are unsaved people. Christians are "not in the flesh but in the Spirit, if in fact the Spirit of God dwells in you" (vs. 9). Then Paul adds, "Anyone who does not have the Spirit of Christ does not belong to him." "The Spirit of Christ" is another name for the Holy Spirit. This is a plain declaration that every Christian has the Holy Spirit dwelling within him. Then he says, "And if Christ is in you." This seems to identify the Holy Spirit and Christ. However, we need to keep in mind that in the mystery of the Trinity, Father, Son and Spirit all dwell within the believer (John 14:17, 23).

The force of verse 10 seems to be, "But if Christ is in you, although the body is dead because of sin, the Spirit is life because of righteousness." Our body is subject to death. Not only is this true, but the body is incapable of righteousness. This is parallel with the passage in Romans 7: "For I know that nothing good dwells in me, that is, in my flesh" (7:18). But we have the righteousness of Christ, and the spirit is alive because of righteousness. There follows the eleventh verse, one of those glorious verses which brings together the work of the Triune

God. The Holy Spirit, the Spirit of the Father who raised up Jesus from the dead, is dwelling in every believer. If that is so, then the Father who raised up Christ from the dead "will also give life to your mortal bodies through his Spirit who dwells in you."

Many devoted Christians have used this verse to teach divine healing, taking the "quickening" to mean the healing of the physical diseases of our mortal bodies. If this were so, it would mean that for the first time in the eight chapters of Romans, Paul suddenly introduces the new idea of the healing of the body, mentions it in one verse, and from that time on dismisses it entirely. It is certainly true that Christians indwelt by the Spirit and walking in the Spirit will be blessed in their physical life. It is not true that healing is in the atonement, in the sense that physical healing may be "claimed" by faith. Great spiritual darkness has come to earnest Christians who have claimed this; some have even doubted that the Holy Spirit was living within them, because their bodily diseases have not healed. There are many methods of healing physical disease: there is surgery, or medicine, or rest, or dieting. Some of the most wicked people in the world have been the healthiest people in the world. But there is only one way of healing sin—through the atonement of our Lord.

Every blessing certainly comes to Christians through the atonement. At the completion of our redemption there will be the resurrection of our bodies. We shall have a body like His. Christians ought not to deny that God can and does heal miraculously, apart from the use of human means. But this does not mean that it is always God's will to heal, for manifestly it is not (Phil. 2:27; 2 Tim. 4:20).

Nearly all interpreters judge that this eleventh verse refers to the resurrection of the body. There are some who have drawn from the statement "through his Spirit who dwells in you," the conclusion that the Holy Spirit is still dwelling within the dust of dead believers, and will give them life at the resurrection. The redemption of our body is the completion of our redemption. The resurrection of Christ from the dead is the sure evidence that we also shall be raised from the dead. But it is evident that here Paul is speaking about present victory. We have been united with Christ in His death. We shall be united with Christ in His resurrection, when we have a body like His. But is there no foretaste of that in the present? Is there no resurrection life for Christians now? Does it not seem clear that this is the main topic of Paul's message here—the present resurrection life? This is not to deny that the resurrection of the body is included as a final completion of salvation. But it is to deny that the present work of the Holy Spirit in believers is excluded. Indeed, this would seem to be the main emphasis. If that is so, Paul is saying that although our bodies are dead because of sin, and that this "mortal body" or this "dead body" is incapable of righteousness (as demonstrated in Romans 7), there is the good news that the indwelling Holy Spirit gives resurrection life to us while we are living in these bodies. We are, therefore, to walk after the Spirit, living by His power.

If we live after the flesh, we must die. That is what unbelievers are doing. To the extent that Christians walk after the flesh, they are walking in the realm of death. Paul is not discussing here whether any Christians can walk after the flesh and be lost eternally. Every child of God will be kept by God's power. Paul is here presenting two opposite kinds of living. Instead of living after the flesh, what are we to do? We are to put to death the doings of the body (vs. 13). This expression, "doings of the body," is used in the sense of the sinful doings, because the desires of the body are in control, and are used contrary to God's will. The natural desires of the body are desires that Adam had before he sinned, desires that our Lord Jesus had.

There are three desires that human beings have, which have been summed up as "the desire to enjoy things, the desire to get things, the desire to do things." The desire to enjoy things has to do with the appetites of our bodies. The desire to get things is related to all that is in the world outside of ourselves. The desire to do things, the ambition to accomplish things, concerns all that we do to affect that world outside ourselves. Temptation strikes at these desires, making an appeal to the man to use the desires contrary to the will of God. When he does that, there results the sins of the lust of the flesh, the lust of the eye, the pride or vainglory of life. When we are controlled by these desires, instead of being controlled by the will of God in the use of our human desires, we have what is here called "the doings of the body." These "doings" may be outward sins, like drunkenness or sexual immorality, or they may be inward sins sometimes called "sins of the spirit," like pride, resentment, selfishness—anything contrary to love. All such are "the doings of the body."

What are we to do with these "doings"? We are to put them to death. But that is not what the verse says. When a man struggles in his own strength to gain the victory over his temptations, there is defeat and failure. But Paul says, "If *by the Spirit* you put to death the deeds of the body, you will live." Thus the message of God's provision for Christian living is: God the Holy Spirit dwelling within the believer. But what is our part in the matter? Is it that we are to use the Holy Spirit, who is the mighty God? Our part is surrender and faith. We are to yield ourselves to God, as Paul has already told us. Then in our day-by-day walk we are to live by the Spirit. We are to put to death the doings of the body by the power of the Spirit. If there is resentment rising in my heart because of injuries done by some foe or by some friend, I am to recognize it as a sinful thing, the work of the flesh, springing out of self. But I cannot control it. God's law is to love that enemy. But "For I have the desire to do what is right, but not the ability to carry it out."

Shall I go on, then, with the resentment growing and coming to full fruitage? Shall I keep it simmering, and struggle against it? No, I am to put it to death. But I am to put it to death not by will power, but "by the Spirit." I am not to ask the Holy Spirit to come into my heart. I know that He is there, and I am to call unto Him for deliverance and then to believe that He is giving the victory.

A veteran missionary from China gave a testimony that strikingly illustrates the application of this truth to daily living. When he entered China he was overwhelmed by the unattractiveness of the Chinese. The dirt and the smells and the spiritual hardness repelled him. He did not love them. Even when he had learned the language the same barrier remained. He knew that as a missionary he must love them. What should he do? He believed the Lord sent him to China, and the Lord knew what he would meet. So he came in prayer and asked God to give him a love for the Chinese. Then he did what we often fail to do when we pray. He thanked God for the answer. He had God's word for it that the love of God had been shed abroad in his heart by the Holy Spirit (Rom. 5:5). He believed God. That is what faith is—taking God at His Word—thanking Him. There was no change in the mission-ary's feeling; yet the problem was solved. The next time he sat before a Chinese audience he looked out over dirty, unattractive, hardened faces. But there sprang up in his heart such a compassion for those people that all the unloveliness disappeared; tears flowed and he rose to speak with a great love flooding his heart for them. He was, by the Spirit, putting to death the doings of the body.

There follows the statement in verse 14: "For all who are led by the

Spirit of God are sons of God." Here is the test as to whether a man is a son of God. Every child of God has the Holy Spirit living within him. Thus, in a true sense, every child of God is "led by the Spirit of God."

Is this, then, a mechanical thing, so that all Christians are the same, differing only in degree, according as it is God's pleasure to sanctify them, one slowly, another swiftly? Regardless of the problem that is raised at every step in our study of the problem of the relationship between God's part and man's part, we know that Christians may be ignorant of this wonderful plan of God to live by the Spirit. This is the occasion of Paul's writing Romans. But suppose Christians pay no attention to Romans? Suppose they do not study and meditate on these things and learn the secret? Will that have a bearing on their lives? It assuredly will. The difference between Christians may be a difference not only of degree, but an absolute difference, between Christians who are living the Christian life according to God's plan, or attempting to live it according to their own plan.

It is quite true that if a man is born again he will in some measure be "led by the Spirit." But his ignorance of this plan will keep him from living in victory as he ought to live. It is not that there is a "second work of grace," in the sense that God does something for Christians subsequent to regeneration, which we call "entire sanctification," or "the baptism of the Spirit," or "the fullness of the Spirit." But it is a spiritual crisis for a Christian who has been ignorant of this glorious truth of living by the power of the indwelling Spirit, when this truth becomes clear to him.

Preparation for Lesson 8

Reading Lesson: Romans 8

Present Victory and Future Glory (8:15-39)

1. Write briefly in your notebook how the eighth chapter of Romans presents the message of our threefold salvation—past, present, future.

2. Notice that Romans 8 presents a remarkable study of the work of the Holy Spirit. In fact, it may be taken as the outstanding chapter on the Holy Spirit in the Bible. What four distinct truths concerning the Holy Spirit are presented in Romans 8? Note the expressions concerning the Spirit connected with each of these truths.

3. Study Romans 8:28, 8:32, 8:37 and their context.

4. What does Romans 8 reveal concerning the second coming of Christ? What is said about the relation between the deliverance of the whole creation and the deliverance of Christians?

5. What three "groanings" are mentioned in Romans 8, as taking place in this present time? When will the groanings end? Why? Read 2 Corinthians 5:2, 4. In what way should Christians groan?

6. What does it mean to be saved "by hope" or "in hope" (vs. 24)? What connection has this with being saved through faith? What is Christian "hope"? How important is it in Christian living?

7. What is the great purpose for the bringing about of which all things are working together for good? What does it mean to be

"more than conquerors"? When are we more than conquerors, in the present or in the future?

8. In what way is Romans 8 a climax of the teaching on God's way of saving men? What would follow naturally in Paul's argument?

Lesson 8

Triumphant Life in the Spirit

Romans 8:14-39

WITNESS OF THE SPIRIT TO OUR PRESENT SONSHIP—8:14-17

One thing that is necessary to living a victorious Christian life is absolute certainty of our sonship. All fear should be cast away. There should be no "spirit of bondage." We are the children of God: "The Spirit himself bears witness with our spirit that we are children of God" (vs. 16). This does not say that the Spirit bears witness "to" our spirits, but "with" our spirit. The thought is that the Holy Spirit, who is the Spirit of the Son as well as the Spirit of the Father, this Holy Spirit indwelling us, says, "Father," and our spirit says, "Father."

I. L. Legters, the beloved leader of Pioneer Missions, had many experiences in dealing with men who were not brought up in Christian homes. When these men prayed, Mr. Legters testified, they always began, "O God." When one of these men accepted Christ as Saviour, he would in every case, without knowing he was doing it, call God his Father. The witness of the Spirit is not some special emotional feeling, though feeling may accompany the witness of the Spirit. The witness results in an inward conviction, the knowledge that God is our Father. Anyone brought up in a Christian home can say, "Our Father." It is a grave wrong for great groups of people who are unsaved to pray together the Lord's Prayer. No one can say "Jesus is Lord" but in the Holy Spirit. No one can call God "Father" except by the Holy Spirit.

97

Anyone can say with his lips "Jesus is Lord," or with his lips he can call God "Father," believing in what is called the universal fatherhood of God. But this would not be the witness of the Spirit. If a Christian doubts his salvation, and is not enjoying the assurance of salvation, it is not because he does not have the witness of the Spirit. Here again the ignorance of Christians may result in their defeat. There are many Christians troubled because they do not have absolute certainty as to their salvation. But one cannot believe the message of salvation by grace for lost sinners in Romans, and the message of abounding grace for the Christian, without having assurance of salvation.

If we are children, then we are heirs, heirs of God and joint-heirs of Christ; not equal heirs, but better than that, joint-heirs. But there follows a qualification: "provided we suffer with him in order that we may also be glorified with him." The thought is that we are joint-heirs both in sharing His sufferings now and His glory in the future.

FUTURE GLORY OF THE SONS OF GOD—8:18-25

We have suggested that Romans 8 sets forth a three-fold salvation: salvation begun, salvation continued and salvation completed. Present salvation includes victory, and it includes suffering. It includes limitations of this body of our humiliation, not yet redeemed. But now Paul brings before us the present power of the truth concerning our future salvation: "For in this hope we were saved" (vs. 24). This does not mean that we hope that we are saved, as so many express it. It means that our salvation includes a great "hope," the glorious future completion of our redemption, and the crowning of Christ as Lord over a restored creation. Thus, we might read this verse, "For we were saved with a great hope in view." Hope in the New Testament never means what we ordinarily mean when we say that "we hope." Our thought of "hope" includes always more or less uncertainty. But this hope is an absolute certainty. But it is in the future, and it is not seen: "Now hope that is seen is not hope. For who hopes for what he sees? But if we hope for what we do not see, we wait for it with patience"(vs. 25). That is, the hope is a certainty and we await it with patience.

This hope is, of course, the Blessed Hope, the Coming in glory of our Lord Himself. It is when He is manifested that the sons of God also shall be manifested in glory (Titus 2:13; Col. 3:4; 1 John 2:28; 3:3).

Paul, recognizing the sufferings of this present time, declares that they are not worthy to be compared with the glory which will be revealed to us. Then he sums up again the great conflict in this present age. He speaks of the whole creation subjected to vanity, in the bondage of corruption, groaning and travailing in pain until now. What a vivid picture of the situation in the world today! It has been the situation since sin entered.

Paul says two things about this great bondage. It had a beginning. It was not always so. It is not inherent in the nature of the creation that it should be so. It was subjected because of sin. The other great truth is that this bondage is not to continue. There is to be a deliverance. The deliverance is connected with "the liberty of the glory of the children of God." The whole creation is lying in the evil one, and is groaning and travailing in pain (1 John 5:19). Men are trying their own plans to solve the problem of war. They are vain plans. Notice this startling statement: "And not only so, but ourselves also." There is a group of people in the world who are utterly separated from all the rest of creation—"ourselves also." What is the difference? This: we are they "who have the firstfruits of the Spirit." Even we are groaning within ourselves. Why? We are waiting for the completion of our salvation, called here "the redemption of our body." The Holy Spirit dwelling within is a foretaste of that future glory.

Here we have, incidentally, an answer to the question as to what a Christian is. A Christian is one who is born of the Spirit and in whom the Holy Spirit is living. We are not able always to tell whether this man or that man is a Christian. We can know that the man who is a Christian has dwelling within him the mighty God—Father, Son and Holy Spirit. The man who is not a Christian is without God and without hope in the world.

However, the emphasis of the teaching here is that the present indwelling of the Holy Spirit is in the nature of firstfruits. We have noted already the three expressions concerning the Holy Spirit which point toward the completion of our salvation. We are "sealed with the Spirit" unto the day of redemption; that is, we have the mark of the ownership of God upon us, even the Holy Spirit. He is "the earnest" of our full inheritance. Present salvation is the enjoyment of the foretaste of that full salvation, which is ours when our body is redeemed and our union with God in Christ is complete. And here in Romans the firstfruits point forward to a completed harvest.

WHILE WAITING, WE HAVE THE SPIRIT FOR PRAYER—8:26-27

In this present stage of our salvation, we are compassed with infirmities. But the Holy Spirit, who is the earnest of our full inheritance, is making intercession for us according to the will of God. What is that will of God? What is His glorious purpose? It is no less than conformity to the image of Christ. That is the goal. And that is the gateway to all the infinite treasures of God throughout eternity.

ALL THINGS WORKING TOWARD HIS GLORIOUS PURPOSE FOR EVERY BELIEVER: CONFORMITY TO THE IMAGE OF CHRIST— 8:28-30

What of the present with its trials and disappointments? All things are now working together for good. Someone has suggested that it does not say for "goods." This assurance is only for those who love God—a love expressed by taking Christ as Saviour and Lord, and living for Him.

There follows a summing up of God's eternal purpose for everyone who is saved. They are those whom "He foreknew." The meaning of this word "foreknew" is not to be found in the truth that God foreknows all that is to come to pass, but rather in the meaning that is given to the word "know" in the matter of salvation. Those who are saved, who love God, are those who are known of God (I Cor. 8:3). Thus, a distinction is drawn between our knowing God, and being "known of God" (Gal. 4:9). This is equivalent to being loved of God: "not that we loved God, but that he loved us" (I John 4:10). When Christ says to those who are rejected, "I never knew you," He does not use that word in the sense of not knowing who they are (Matt. 7:23). He certainly knew who they were. That is the reason He is condemning them. He means that He never knew them with approval as those who belong to Himself (Luke 13:24-30). So this word "foreknow" refers to those whom God has previously approved, or chosen for Himself. Apart from the question of how He chooses, or on what ground He chooses, this seems to be the thought of the message. We know that this includes all those who ultimately will be saved. Each one of these has been foreordained or predetermined by God to be conformed to the image of His Son. That is the goal of God's plan for each one.

This is what salvation means—union with God through Christ. Thus Christ is the first-born among many brethren. He is the Captain or "Founder" of our salvation (Heb. 2:10). How glorious beyond our conception is this view! Carrying out this plan, God called each one of those who was thus ordained. Then He justified them, declared them righteous in Christ. This is summing up what Paul has already described as God's plan of giving righteousness. Then he goes from this righteousness or justification to the culmination of what we call sanctification, or making holy: "those he also glorified." When we have a body like Christ, then is our redemption complete. We are glorified. Since no one is yet glorified, we can see clearly that these words are not speaking of something that has been done, but describing what is God's plan and what is the process for every saved man.

THEREFORE, MORE THAN CONQUERORS—8:31-39

It would appear now that all has been said, and the question follows: "What then shall we say to these things? If God is for us, who can be against us?" Is there anything for the Christian to fear? Is there anything for him to long for which he does not have? There follows another of these gems of the eighth chapter, Romans 8:32: "He who did not spare his own Son but gave him up for us all, how will he not also with him graciously give us all things?" The answer to this question is that since God gave Christ to die for us on the Cross, God will not withhold any lesser blessing. His Son includes all else. He gives us Christ, and with Christ He freely gives us all things. What a fulfillment of the Old Testament's promise: "Those who seek the Lord lack no good thing!" (Ps. 34:10).

But what about tribulation, or anguish, or persecution, or famine, or nakedness, or peril, or sword? Can any of these things separate us from the love of Christ? Are we to judge the love of Christ by the tribulation and suffering that He permits to come to us? Or are we to judge the tribulation and persecution and suffering of every kind in the light of what we know about Christ? The answer is: "No, in all these things we are more than conquerors through him who loved us" (vs. 37). We may conquer an obstacle by having it removed, or by passing around the obstacle. But when we use those very obstacles for greater vision and greater blessing, and greater glory of God, then are we more than conquerors. The wonder of this promise is that we are more than conquerors "in all these things." Our thought usually is that we shall be conquerors when we get rid of the present tribulations and hindrances, especially our own limitations. But no! Christ's victory for us is here and now, where we are. Not in spite of these obstacles, but even because of them, we are "more than conquerors."

The ground of our confidence is the love of God, which is in Christ Jesus our Lord. Let us not look at our own imperfect expression of love for Him. Let us stand on the solid rock of His love to us. That means to look to Calvary. That means to sum up all the glory that Paul has revealed, of grace abounding for the lost sinner, and grace abounding for the saint.

Preparation for Lesson 9

Reading Lesson: Romans 9-10

Israel and the Gospel: The Jew and the Gentile

    A. *What God thinks of Israel* (9:1-6)

        1.   List nine things mentioned in verses 4 and 5.

        2.   Are these things "the gifts and the calling of God" that are not repented of (Rom. 11:29)? If so, how will they be fulfilled in the future? Are the Jews of our day lost?

        3.   Is Paul's sorrow for Israel a type of what our sorrow should be? Why does Paul feel as he does toward Israel? Could Paul be accursed from Christ?

    B. *The Meaning of the Election of Grace* (9:6-30)

        4.   In what way does Paul say God's purposes are fulfilled, although Israel as a whole has rejected its Saviour? (vs. 6-8).

        5.   What "election" is spoken of here (vs. 11), an election of some individuals to salvation and some to ruin, or an election of servants through whom salvation is to be proclaimed?

        6.   When God "hardened Pharaoh's heart," does this mean that God by His decree made Pharaoh a bad man and then punished him for being bad? If not, what does it mean? In what sense did God hate Esau (vs. 13)?

        7.   In verses 23-33 what relationship is shown between Jews and Gentiles and the Gospel?

    C. *Law and Grace: Jew and Gentile* (9:33 - 10:21)

        8.   Was the Gospel of salvation by grace preached by Moses in the Old Testament? What was that Gospel? How did the Jews receive it?

9. In what way is Christ "the end of the law" (vs.4)?

10. In what things are Jews and Gentiles alike? In what things has there been a difference?

11. Do these two chapters say that God has nothing further to do with Israel except with the remnant who, along with the Gentiles, have accepted the Christ? Read 11:11, 25-29.

12. What is the missionary message and appeal in chapter 10?

Details of Chapters 9 to 11

GRACE ABOUNDING FOR THE WORLD—9:11–11:36

God's Missionary Plan for tile World through Jew, Gentile and Church. Key Verses: 11:12 and 11:32.

1. Relation of Israel to the Gospel—9:1-29.

    a. Salvation is of the Jews, yet they are lost—9:1-5

    b. But the spiritual seed is not lost, and through them God's purpose is fulfllled—9:6-24.

    c. This remnant of Israel is joined with the called from among the Gentiles in carrying out God's plan—9:24-29.

2. The Jews reject and the Gentiles receive the Gospel —9:30-10:21.

    a. Gentiles attain to righteousness of faith Israel follows the righteousness of the law— 9:30- 10:10.

    b. The message of faith was preached to Jew and Gentiles alike—10:11-15.

    c. The Jews rejected it, and the Gentiles are now receiving it—10:16.21.

3. Gods election of both Israel and the Church is that the whole world might be reached through them as His Instruments—11:1-32.

    a. What Israel as a whole lost, the remnant who accepted grace obtained—11:1-10.

    b. b. Israel's fall brought great blessing to the Gentiles: their return will mean exceeding blessing for the whole world—11:11-16.

c.   Gentiles (the Church in which Gentiles predominated) stand by faith or fall by unbelief, just as in the case of Israel—11:17-24.

d.   "All Israel shall be saved"—11:25-29.

e.   God's purpose: that He might have mercy upon all—11:30-32.

f.   Climax of praise for God's glorious love plan of salvation for the world—11:33-36.

Lesson 9

Grace Abounding for the World

ROMANS 9:1–11:36

GOD'S MISSIONARY PLAN FOR THE WORLD: FOR JEW AND GENTILE

The eighth chapter ends with a glorious note of triumph over God's love for His trusting children. The ninth opens with a heartbroken expression of God's love for His people who have rejected Him. The eighth chapter has brought us to a climax of salvation, the glorification of the saint in Christ. What is there to follow that?

From Romans 9 to 11 Paul is dealing with Israel. The Jews have considered that if this new message of salvation by grace which Paul has been proclaiming is true, then God's plan for Israel must have been set aside. What is the place of Israel in God's plan of redemption? Paul clearly answers this question in these three chapters. Many interpreters have, therefore, called these chapters a parenthesis. They regard the climax as coming at the end of the eighth chapter, and this parenthesis as explaining how Israel fits into that plan.

It is quite true that the chapters tell how Israel fits into the plan of redemption. But is Israel a parenthesis? If the suggested outline of Romans is a true interpretation, then Romans 9 to 11, instead of being a parenthesis, is one of the most glorious climaxes in the Word of God. If we have a self-centered view of salvation, we may naturally think that the climax of everything is when our own individual ministry on earth is finished, and we go to be with Christ. Following that there is the other great climax, the personal return of Christ, when we shall have a resurrection body like His. But that is not the end of Paul's setting forth of God's plan of redemption. He has told of grace abounding for the lost sinner. He has set forth grace abounding for the saint. Now logically must follow the message of grace abounding for the world.

This does not mean that there is a different Gospel. It does mean that he is setting forth God's missionary plan for the world. What is to be the result of proclaiming this message of grace abounding for the lost sinner, and the message of grace abounding for the saved sinner?

One of the keys to understanding Paul's message of Romans is the expression found in the key verses: "To the Jew first, and also to the Greek." Our Lord Himself said, "Salvation is of the Jews." Some have suggested that the words "to the Jew first, and also to the Greek" (or the Gentile) mean that we should first preach the Gospel to the Jews who are in any city that we enter. This would be a misinterpretation of the verse, and might lead to bondage in the matter of evangelization, even though we should applaud the eager desire to reach the Jews and not neglect them so utterly as they are neglected in our plans for evangelization. But the words "to the Jew first, also to the Gentiles" have a far richer meaning. Israel as God's chosen people was chosen from the beginning for the specific purpose of blessing all the nations of the earth. Israel is never an end in herself. She is always the means to an end, and that end is the blessing of all the nations of the earth.

In approaching Romans 9 to 11, we come to the heart of the great dispute among devoted students of the Word as to the place of Israel in God's plan of redemption. What is the future of Israel? What bearing does Israel have on the Second Coming of our Lord?

Three answers have been given to this question by Bible interpreters, although there are many variations of each of these three views.

The first is that sometime in the future, during this present age of grace, Israel as a nation will accept Christ through the preaching of the Gospel. This great event will probably mark the beginning of a new era of universal peace, and the triumph of the Gospel for a long period of time. This period is identified with the thousand years or the millennium. After that period, Christ will return, and so this view is called the postmillennial view of Christ's coming.

Second, there is the view that Israel as a nation, or a large part of the Israelites, will accept Christ as Saviour, probably at the moment when He returns. They will then be instantly caught up to be with Christ, as other believers. This will close the present age, and will mark the destruction of the world, and the creation of the new heavens and the new earth. This will inaugurate the eternal state, no millennial age of peace on the earth intervening. This is called the amillennial view, although not all amillenarians would believe that Israel is saved at the appearing of Christ. Some would interpret "all Israel" to mean the completed number of Jews who are going to accept Christ, and they take the view that these Israelites will be saved through the preaching of the Gospel in this present age.

The third view is that Israel as a nation will be saved at the appearing of the Lord, and will remain on earth to be a blessing to all the nations of the world during the period called the millennium. This is the premilliennial view of Christ's return.

Paul says plainly, in Romans 11:26, "And in this way all Israel will be saved." It will be seen that all three of these views accept the fact that there will yet be such a conversion of Jews as to be designated as "all Israel." The very fact that there are millions of Jews on the earth, even after the terrible slaughter of the World War years, indicates that God has a purpose for these Jews as Jews. What is that purpose?

We know that Messiah came through Israel. We know that in this age the middle wall of partition has been broken down. Both Jews and Gentiles are saved by grace through faith. Paul has emphasized this great truth in Romans. Why should the Jews as Jews continue? This is a serious problem for those who maintain that all the prophecies of the Old Testament concerning Israel are intended to be taken figuratively or spiritually, and are fulfilled in the Church. If that were so, the natural course of events would be to have the Jews as Jews disappear and be amalgamated with the Gentiles; but they are here, and this constitutes a problem. Paul deals with this in Romans 9 to 11. What is his answer?

SALVATION IS OF THE JEWS, YET THEY ARE LOST—9:1-5

Paul's compassionate love for his brethren is but an expression of God's love poured out in Paul's heart. Saul of Tarsus had been breathing out threats and slander from every fiber of his being against the followers of the Lord Jesus. Oh, what a change! He is now breathing out love for the Jewish people who were seeking to murder him, and such love that he can express it only in the hyperbolic form of wishing that he himself were accursed from Christ for his brethren's sake. Think of the glory of Israel, to whom were committed the oracles of God, to whom was revealed the service of worship, to whom were given the promises of redemption and the covenants of God, to whom belonged the fathers, Abraham, Isaac and Jacob, and the others. The chief glory of Israel: "of whom is Christ as concerning the flesh," the One who is "God blessed forever." What a tragedy that Israel should be in such a state of blindness after her manifold blessings!

BUT THE SPIRITUAL SEED IS NOT LOST, AND THROUGH THEM GOD'S PURPOSE IS FULFILLED—9:6-24

The natural question in the minds of the Jew is whether God's Word has come to nothing, for Israel has rejected Christ. Paul's answer to this is plain and positive. That rejection by Israel was not complete. The believing remnant did not reject Messiah, but received Him. He seems to be going to the length of saying that the Israel that rejected Christ is not Israel at all: "For not all who are descended from Israel belong to Israel." As is his custom, he goes back to the Old Testament revelation to show that God's call of Israel was a matter of His own sovereign grace. God chose Isaac, not Ishmael, although Ishmael was also Abraham's seed. God also chose Jacob and not Esau, although Esau was the son of both Rebecca and Sarah, and the twin brother of Jacob.

When facing the mystery of God's electing grace, a mystery that goes far beyond our understanding, we need to keep in mind both sides. It was by grace that God chose Jacob. But all the facts about Jacob and Esau and all the facts of history indicate that it was the right choice. In other words, we should never think of God's foreordaining grace in human terms, as though God were predetermining things in the arbitrary way in which we would do. There is no avoiding the fact that in this ninth chapter of Romans Paul is teaching sovereign election. At the same time, we need to remember that he is not here dealing with the question of the salvation of individual souls, but rather with the question of God's use of Israel, and the meaning of Israel's rejection of Christ. They had challenged Paul's Gospel. Paul at one time rejected Christ because he believed He did not fulfill the Old Testament prophecies. When he met the risen Lord and was illumined with regard to his own Scriptures, he could say, as he said before King

Agrippa, "To this day I have had the help that comes from God, and so I stand here testifying both to small and great, saying nothing but what the prophets and Moses said would come to pass: that the Christ must suffer and that, by being the first to rise from the dead, he would proclaim light both to our people and to the Gentiles" (Acts 26:22-23).

Thus, he is showing that the Gospel is exactly what the Old Testament prophesied. God is dealing in grace, and mercy, and compassion: "I will have mercy on whom I have mercy, and I will have compassion on whom I have compassion." But what of those whom God hardened? Pharaoh is an example. The hardening of Pharaoh's heart does not mean that God made Pharaoh a bad man, and then punished him for being bad. Pharaoh hardened his own heart. God raised him up, and He did it for the great purpose of mercy, "that I might show my power in you, and that my name might be proclaimed in all the earth. So then he has mercy on whomever he wills, and he hardens whomever he wills." We remember the climax of his argument: "So then he has mercy on whomever he wills, and he hardens whomever he wills" (11:32).

THE REMNANT OF ISRAEL IS JOINED WITH THE CALLED GENTILES IN CARRYING OUT GOD'S PLAN—9:24-29

God's plan, then, is to make known the riches of His glory "upon vessels of mercy, which he afore prepared unto glory." These, Paul declares, are not from the Jews only, but also from the Gentiles. Then he quotes a passage from Hosea which originally referred to the Jews, but which Paul now by the Spirit applies also to the Gentiles, "Those who were not my people I will call 'my people,' and her who was not beloved I will call 'beloved.'" "And in the very place where it was said to them, 'You are not my people,' there they will be called 'sons of the living God'" (9:25-26). Thus this promise of the restoration of Israel includes the salvation of the Gentiles. He quotes Isaiah: "It is the remnant that will be saved" (9:27). What has happened with regard to the rejection of Christ by Israel as a nation, and the acceptance of Christ by the remnant of Israel, is in accordance with the Old Testament prophecies.

GENTILES ATTAIN TO RIGHTEOUSNESS OF FAITH, ISRAEL FOLLOWS THE RIGHTEOUSNESS OF THE LAW—9:30-10:10

Paul sums up the case as it stands between Jews and Gentiles: "That Gentiles who did not pursue righteousness have attained it, that is, a righteousness that is by faith" (9:30). This, of course, refers to Gentiles who have accepted Christ as Saviour, not to the Gentiles as a whole. While Israel was God's people in the Old Testament, He let the Gentile nations go their own way. Individuals from the Gentiles accepted the true God and became proselytes of Israel. But as a whole, the Gentiles were not seeking after God's righteousness. Now, under the Gospel, they are attaining it, not by works of the law, but by faith, even as Paul has been explaining in this letter to the Romans. But Israel, following after a law of righteousness, "did not succeed in reaching that law" (9:31) — that is, Israel did not attain to righteousness. Yet Israel had the law, which was the setting forth of God's righteousness. Why did they not obtain it? The answer is clear.

When we read this answer, it may be well to keep in mind the teaching that has been accepted by many, that Israel mistakenly put herself under the law when she said, "All that the Lord has spoken we will do, and we will be obedient." Israel was not saying, "We will be obedient as the condition of our salvation." Israel was never under law as a means of salvation. No human being was ever under law as a means of salvation. The only other thing that Israel could have said was: "We will not obey these laws that God has given us." That law was not given them as a means of salvation, but as a rule of life for a redeemed people. They were already under the blood. This does not mean that every individual really had faith in his heart and was saved. But Israel was God's people under the blood, that is, under grace, looking forward to a Redeemer. Meanwhile, they were to keep this law of God which was a special dispensation imposed upon them until the Redeemer Himself should come.

What was the mistake of Israel? Was it the mistake of putting themselves under law, a mistake which God permitted? Paul does not say so. He says, "Because they did not pursue it by faith, but as if it were based on works" (9:32). Pursue what? Pursue righteousness. How should they have pursued it? By faith. That is the teaching of the Old Testament. Paul's text, "The righteous will live by faith," is an Old Testament text. Abraham believed God, and it was counted to him for righteousness. David and all those in his generation who were saved were justified by grace through faith. The Jews made a mistake by turning away from God's plan, not by following something which God permitted. They chose something which God forbade. They were seeking to establish their own righteousness. They stumbled at the stone of stumbling; that is, they rejected the crucified and risen Saviour.

But let us mark it very clearly that the believing remnant of Israel did not so reject Christ. Abraham, Isaac, Jacob, Joseph, Samuel, David, Isaiah, Jeremiah and Ezekiel did not stumble at the stone of stumbling. They arrived at righteousness by faith. So did every other humble Jew, including the seven thousand in Elijah's day that had not bowed the knee to Baal. All through the history of Israel there was a remnant according to the election of grace. This remnant, including Paul himself, accepted Messiah.

Paul is not discussing this whole matter from a cold intellectual standpoint. Theology to him goes to the very heart of life, for he interrupts his argument by crying, "Brethren, my heart's desire and prayer to God for them is that they may be saved" (Rom. 10:1). Then the Jews are lost. Let this great fact burn into our hearts in these days when blind Protestants are linking Catholics, Jews and Protestants together as the people of God, all believing in the true God, and all seeking the right way. But do not the Jews believe in the true God? Paul says, "For I bear them witness that they have a zeal for God, but not according to knowledge." They are ignorant of God's righteousness. But that is what salvation is—God's righteousness. They are seeking to establish their own righteousness. Therefore, they did not subject themselves to the righteousness of God.

The Jews had the law. What was that law? It was God's message of salvation to them. What confusion is thrown upon all the teaching of the Gospel when we get the idea that the poor Jews were under law and therefore did not know the wonderful message of salvation by grace through faith! Paul says they rejected that message which was the whole purpose of the revelation that was given to them.

Moses preached righteousness by grace through faith. In the marvelous passage in Deuteronomy 30:11-20 he pleads with Israel to love God with their whole heart. The commandment is not too hard, not far off: "But the word is very near you. It is in your mouth and in your heart, so that you can do it." This is the passage Paul quotes as to what the righteousness of faith says. He gives the clearer light of the New Testament of what faith means. We do not need someone to ascend into heaven to bring the Messiah down. We confess that Jesus is the Christ. He has come from heaven. But He died and was buried! We do not need someone to descend to bring Christ up. He has risen! So we confess that Jesus is the Saviour and Lord and we believe in our heart that God has raised Him from the dead.

But Israel stumbled at this Old Testament message of faith. They sought righteousness the hard way, the impossible way, by works, trying to keep the outward ordinances. The Gentiles, who never followed after righteousness, are entering in by faith—that is, many from among them are. "A righteousness of my own" (Phil. 3:9), Paul calls the righteousness that is of the law, and he contrasts it with the righteousness which is from God by faith: keeping outward ordinances is my own way of righteousness; trusting Jesus Christ is God's way, and results in heart righteousness that keeps the righteous requirements of the law in the measure in which we are controlled by the Holy Spirit.

The summing up of this whole message is in Romans 10:4, although our English translation may obscure the central truth: "For Christ is the end of the law for righteousness to everyone who believes." Some suppose this means that when Christ came, the law came to an end. But the whole tenor of the argument would favor the meaning: "The purpose or intent of the law is, Christ for righteousness, to everyone who believes." Righteousness cannot come through the law. But the law, Paul has said, witnesses to the Saviour. The law is a pedagogue unto Christ in the sense that the whole Mosaic revelation had as its purpose or intent or end, "Christ for righteousness."

THE MESSAGE OF FAITH WAS PREACHED TO JEW AND GENTILE ALIKE—10:11-21

Paul stresses again the universal *whosoever* of the Gospel:

"everyone who calls on the name of the Lord will be saved." Again he presses home the fact that "there is no distinction between Jew and Greek." Then follow those searching missionary questions. We ask the question as to what God is going to do with the heathen who never heard of Christ. But we should hear God's questions. This passage clearly teaches that only those who look to the Lord Jesus Christ can be saved. They must believe in Him. But to believe in Him, they must hear about Him. To hear about Him, they must have a preacher. Therefore, the preacher must be sent. This has been true from the very beginning. It is a solemn truth that there is no salvation except through the Lord Jesus Christ, and God has no plan for bringing this salvation to men except through human beings who are chosen of Him as preachers: "As it is written, How beautiful are the feet of those who preach the good news!"

God's heart still goes out to Israel, and the very acceptance of the Gospel by the Gentiles He uses to provoke the Jews to a wholesome jealousy.

Preparation for Lesson 10

Reading Lesson: Romans 9–11

Note: Romans 11 is one of the most important prophetic chapters in the New Testament. It answers directly the important question as to whether God still has a plan for the Jews as a nation or whether all their prophecies are fulfilled through the spiritual "Israel of God"—the believers in Christ from both Jews and Gentiles. Unless this question is answered correctly, most of the prophetic portions of Scripture must remain a puzzle.

A. *Israel Failed, But the Remnant Win the Promises* (11:1-10)

1. What does Paul mean by the casting off of God's people? Why does he give himself and the seven thousand who did not bow the knee to Baal, in Elijah's time, as proofs that God did not cast off His people?

2. Who were "the remnant according to the election of grace" in Paul's day? Does he mean that through them were fulfilled all God's promises to Israel?

3. What did God do to the rest of Israel who were not in the "election of grace"? Why did He act that way toward them? What kept them out of the remnant (vs. 20)?

B. *What God Did through the Fall of Israel* (11:11-24)

1. What does the question in verse 11 mean: "Did they stumble that they might fall?"

2. What did Paul do each time the Jews rejected the Gospel that he preached? Read Acts 13:46; 18:6; 22:17-21; 28:24-28. What

does he say in Romans 11 was the result of this rejection by the Jews (vs. 15)?

3. Do these verses mean that a Christian may turn to unbelief and be lost? If not, what does it mean to have the branches broken off the olive tree?

C. *The Great Prophecy of Israel's Future Salvation* (11:25-36)

1. Does the prophecy that "all Israel shall be saved" refer to the spiritual "Israel" or to the Jews as a nation? What is meant by the "a partial hardening" and by "the fullness of the Gentiles" (vs. 25)?

2. How did God "shut up all unto disobedience"? On how many people does God choose to have mercy?

3. Why is this prophecy about Israel so important to God's plan of salvation for the world as to call forth the great praise in verses 33 to 36? What do these verses mean? What do they reveal about the Trinity? Compare with 1 Cor. 8:6; Col. 1:16; Heb. 2:10.

4. How is God's missionary plan for the world revealed in Romans 9 to 11?

Israel and the Church

Romans 11:1-32

WHAT ISRAEL AS A WHOLE LOST, THE REMNANT WHO ACCEPTED GRACE OBTAINED—11:1-10

To this question as to whether God's promises to Israel had failed, in view of the fact that Israel rejected her Messiah, Paul gives this clear and direct answer. The rejection by Israel was not complete. The believing remnant of Israel, including Paul and the twelve apostles, and the three thousand at Pentecost, and the many thousands who afterward believed, did not reject Messiah. This believing remnant constituted the true Israel. Through them, Paul says, God's promises are fulfilled.

But this is not the whole answer to the question. If it were, there would seem no reason why the Jews as Jews should continue on earth. In that case Israel's work has been finished. Those thousands who accepted Christ ceased to be Jews. They ceased to be Jews not only because they were made one with the Gentiles in the Body of Christ, but they intermarried with the Gentiles and disappeared as Jews. If all God's promises in the Old Testament to Israel as a nation are fulfilled spiritually in the Church of Christ, composed of Jews and Gentiles, there is no future for Israel as a nation. Individual Jews indeed will be saved, but they are on the same basis as individual Gentiles. When they take Christ as their Saviour, they are united with the Body of Christ, where there is neither Jew nor Greek.

But Paul has another very important answer to the question concerning the rejection of Messiah by Israel. That rejection was not complete, but he also makes clear in the climax of his argument that that rejection is not final. God does have a future for Israel as Israel, and as a nation. From some of Paul's expressions as to who are the true Israel, one might gather that God is through with the Israel which has rejected Him. It is the neglecting or the ignoring of one or other of these answers of Paul which leads to wrong views about the future of Israel and the coming of Christ. On the one hand, there are those who say that all the prophecies of the Old Testament were fulfilled, or are being fulfilled, or will be fulfilled through the Church. They ignore the second message that the rejection by Israel was not final. Again there are those who say that none of the prophecies of the Old Testament concerning Israel are fulfilled in the Church, and all those prophecies, they say, are for the future. They ignore the plain teaching that the rejection by Israel was not complete. The truth must be found in the fact that many of the prophecies of the Old Testament were fulfilled and are being fulfilled through the remnant of Israel, but that the complete fulfillment of these same prophecies, and the clear fulfillment of other prophecies, are in the future, and will be fulfilled through Israel as a nation.

Let us study Paul's teaching concerning this truth that the rejection by Israel of their Messiah is not final.

ISRAEL'S FALL BROUGHT BLESSING TO THE GENTILES: THEIR RETURN WILL MEAN EXCEEDING BLESSING FOR THE WHOLE WORLD—11:11-16

He asks, "did they stumble in order that they might fall?" (11:11).

He then repels this suggestion. If the Jews did stumble at the stumbling stone and rejected Christ "that they might fall," it would mean that the story was at an end. The final word has been spoken about Israel as a nation. They have rejected God. God has rejected them. The believing portion of them received the Messiah, and through them all God's promises are fulfilled. But this is precisely the conclusion which Paul rejects, and rejects with that strong expression in the English translation, "God forbid!" By this fall of Israel, by this rejection of their Messiah, "salvation has come to the Gentiles." This cannot mean that Gentiles are saved because Israel rejected the Messiah. Gentiles are saved by grace, through faith in the crucified and risen Saviour. But he is speaking here of Israel as a group, and the Gentiles as a group. He is explaining the new dispensation. Our Lord Himself said that the kingdom of God was to be taken away from the Jews and given to a nation bearing the fruits thereof (Matt. 21:43). This nation is the Church, using the word "nation" in a figurative sense, or a spiritual sense, as Peter does when he speaks of "a chosen race, a royal priesthood, a holy nation, a people for his own possession" (I Pet. 2:9). But observe also that salvation has come to the Gentiles, not in the sense of rejecting and punishing the Jews, but "to provoke them to jealousy."

Nevertheless, the fall of Israel was the occasion of the riches of the Gentile world. The passing of Judaism and destruction of their temple, which seemed such a tragedy to them, blossomed out in the glory of the Gospel age. It was indeed the riches of the world. Is this the end of the story for Israel? Paul answers, "Now if their trespass means riches for the world, and if their failure means riches for the Gentiles, how much more will their full inclusion mean?" (11:12). What does Paul mean by "their fullness"? He is going on to explain that the rejection by Israel was not final. They are going to receive their Messiah. What

will be the result of that? Much more riches for the Gentiles! Paul
mentions that he is an apostle to the Gentiles, but how his heart is
yearning for Israel. He wants to save them. Then comes the declaration: "For if their rejection means the reconciliation of the world, what
will their acceptance mean but life from the dead?" (11:15). Here it is
clearly implied that Israel is going to be received. This cannot apply
to individual Jews that are saved, because all of the believing remnant
were saved. It refers to those who were cast away. The casting away of
Israel as a nation was the occasion of the reconciling of the world, that
is, bringing the whole world, Jew and Gentile, into this new Gospel
dispensation. This, of course, does not refer to the conversion of the
world, but to this remarkable change from what we may call the Jewish
dispensation to the dispensation of the Church. But what will be the
result of receiving of Israel as a nation? Paul cannot describe it, and
he says, "life from the dead."

GENTILES (THE CHURCH IN WHICH GENTILES PREDOMI-NATE) STAND BY FAITH OR FALL BY UNBELIEF, AS IN THE CASE OF ISRAEL—11:17-24

Paul goes on to explain the relationship between the Jews that were
rejected and the Gentiles who were received, by using the figure of the
olive tree. He says, "Some of the branches were broken off," referring
to the Jews who had rejected Messiah. This mild expression "some"
is occasionally used in Scripture when it refers not to a few but to a
great number. (cf. 1 Tim. 4:1: "some will depart from the faith.") Then
he refers to the Gentiles as branches from a wild olive grafted into the
olive tree, among the believing Israelites.

Some would judge that the olive tree represents Israel. Others would say that the olive tree represents Christ, and that the branches, whether Jews or Gentiles, are joined to Christ. Perhaps this question does not need to be decided in a precise way, inasmuch as the olive tree is both the root and the branches. The truth is that Israel is God's own olive tree. It is the Gentiles who when they became partakers of Christ became partakers of Israel's blessing.

This truth is made clear in Ephesians, the book that deals especially with the mystery of the Church and of our union with Christ. The uncircumcision, or the Gentiles, were once "separated from Christ, alienated from the commonwealth of Israel and strangers to the covenants of promise, having no hope and without God in the world." (Eph. 2:12). Paul tells of that mystery which was not previously made known, "as it has now been revealed to his holy apostles and prophets by the Spirit" (Eph. 3:5). Some say that only Paul had this revelation. Here Paul distinctly declares that it was made known to His holy apostles and prophets. This does not mean that Paul made it known to them, but that God revealed it in the Spirit.

What is that mystery? Some say that it was the mystery of the Church, or the mystery that the Gentiles were to be saved. The word "mystery" does not mean something mysterious, but something which until now has been hidden and needs to be revealed. The godly Jews never had any question about the fact that God wanted the Gentiles saved. Even the unbelieving Jews compassed land and earth that they might make one proselyte. Peter and the others were perfectly clear about the fact that Gentiles were to be saved as well as Jews. What they were not clear about is that Gentiles were not to become Jews when they were saved. A new order was coming. Paul expresses it, "that the Gentiles are fellow heirs, members of the same body, and partakers of the promise in Christ Jesus through the gospel." (Eph. 3:6). Paul was exhorting the Gentiles of his day, "do not become proud, but fear." Gentiles need that same exhortation today. Their general thought is that the Church is a Gentile matter and by sufferance we do allow the Jews to come in and partake of the glory of the Gospel which we have in Christ, and which Israel rejected. The case, Paul explains, is the precise opposite of that. It is we who are sharing this fatness of the olive tree, which was peculiarly Israel's. However, we are "fellow-heirs." It is not that the Jews now have a superiority.

Many who have been zealous to maintain the rights of Israel in obtaining the blessing promised in the Old Testament have taught that the Church had nothing to do with Israel. They illustrated by saying that Israel was like the train on the track of redemption which was switched to a side track. A new train called the Church, a mystery never mentioned in the Old Testament, is now on the track. When the Church is raptured, and Christ returns, this train Israel, on the side track, will be switched back on the main track.

Dr. G. Allen Fleece tells of an incident in his seminary days, when he was explaining to a group of students this relationship between Israel and the Church, using the illustration of the train. One of the students, a quiet, thoughtful fellow who was the son of a missionary, asked, "How about the illustration of the olive tree?"

"What is that?" Dr. Fleece asked.

The missionary's son explained about the olive tree, the branches that were broken off, representing Israel who had rejected Christ, and the branches from the wild olive tree grafted in, representing the Gentiles.

Dr. Fleece, in his thoughtful manner, considered for a while and then said, "I like my illustration better!"

Some weeks later when he was reading through Romans he came

across this illustration of the olive tree.

The missionary's son dropped the matter and did not embarrass his fellow student by telling him that this was not his illustration, but one that the Holy Spirit gave to Paul. Dr. Fleece has now changed his illustration, and says that the same train is on the same track, but many passengers, representing the Jews who rejected Messiah, have gotten off the train, and many other passengers, namely, the Gentiles, have boarded the train.

However, the main point of Paul's argument here is to prove that these branches that were broken off would be grafted in again: "for God has the power to graft them in again." (11:23). He makes this argument very strong by referring to the fact that if Gentiles were cut out of that which is by nature a wild olive tree, and grafted contrary to nature into a good olive tree, "how much more" will the Jews, the natural branches, be grafted into their own olive tree? Observe that Paul is not here speaking of individual salvation, and of the question as to whether a man can be lost and then saved again. He is speaking of Israel which, as a nation, has rejected Christ, and of the Gentiles as over against Israel.

"ALL ISRAEL SHALL BE SAVED"—11:25-29

Thus far, Paul has not declared definitely that these branches will be grafted in again. He says that God is able to do it. He suggests that they need not continue in their unbelief.

But now he comes to the glorious revelation of another "mystery," that is something which has not yet been revealed. "A hardening in part hath befallen Israel" (11:25). He still reminds them that the believing remnant of Israel has not been hardened, but that the others have been hardened. But this hardening will continue only "until the fullness of the Gentiles has come in." Then follows the glorious declaration, "And in this way all Israel will be saved."

As in the case of all important declarations of Scripture, several different interpretations have been given to this expression "all Israel." All who accept God's Word, of course, believe that whatever it means, "all Israel will be saved." Some take "all Israel" as referring to all of the Jews who during the Gospel age will be gathered in through the proclamation of the Gospel by the Church, which would be largely through the Gentiles.

Dr. David Brown, who in his lifetime was considered the leading scholar among postmillennial writers, and one of the authors of the famous Jamieson, Fausset and Brown Commentary, has this comment on the meaning of "all Israel will be saved": "To understand this great statement, as some still do, merely of such a gradual bringing of individual Jews, that there shall at length remain none in unbelief, is to do manifest violence both to it and to the whole context. It can only mean the ultimate ingathering of Israel as a nation, in contrast with the present 'remnant.'" Then he adds. "So, Tholuck, Meyer, Dewette, Philippi, Alford, Hodge." This comment is quoted because Dr. Brown, as opposed to premillennialism, would be likely to do away with the force of this great statement that "all Israel will be saved." Doubtless, names of other great commentators could be given as against this interpretation. But we do not need great interpreters to tell us that the whole subject of Paul's discussion here is the believing remnant of Israel as over against the natural Israel, the Israel that has rejected Christ. However, they are to be saved; whatever the manner of their salvation, there seems to be no question that this salvation of Israel refers to Israel as a nation, and is in contrast to, and separate from, the other great truth that individual Jews were saved in Paul's day and continue to be saved all through this present age.

Paul distinctly declares, "As regards the gospel, they are enemies for your sake." He is thus speaking of the Jews who have rejected Christ; "But as regards election, they are beloved for the sake of their forefathers." He is speaking here of the nation of Israel which has rejected Messiah. Then he adds, "For the gifts and the calling of God are irrevocable." Here again, we might quote Dr. Brown, the postmillennialist: "And lest any should say that though Israel, as a nation, has no destiny at all under the Gospel, but as a people disappeared from the stage when the middle wall of partition was broken down, yet the Abrahamic covenant still endures in the spiritual seed of Abraham, made up of Jews and Gentiles in one undistinguished mass of redeemed men under the Gospel—the apostle, as if to preclude that supposition, expressly states that the very Israel who, as concerning the Gospel, are regarded as 'enemies for the Gentiles sakes,' are 'beloved for the fathers' sake'; and it is in proof of this that he adds, 'for the gifts and the calling of God are without repentance.' In other words, the natural Israel, not 'the remnant of them according to the election of grace,' but the nation, sprung from Abraham according to the flesh—are still an elect people, and as such, beloved."

GOD'S PURPOSE: THAT HE MIGHT HAVE MERCY UPON ALL —11:30-36

Then Paul sums up by addressing the Gentiles, "For just as you were at one time disobedient to God but now have received mercy because of their disobedience, so they too have now been disobedient in order that by the mercy shown to you they also may now receive mercy." These verses make it clear that Paul does not speak of the individuals to whom he is writing, as individual believers, but he is explaining the great plan of God to bring salvation to the Jew first, and then to the Gentiles, explaining the difference between the age in which the kingdom of God was first committed to Israel, now in this age committed to the Church: "For God has consigned all to disobedience, that he may have mercy on all," that is, have mercy on both Jews and Gentiles.

Now comes the glorious climax of this passage on grace abounding for the world. It is the plan that only the mind of God could conceive, and only the love and power of God could bring to pass. He is declaring here that all things come from God the Father as the Source of all things, and all things come through God the Son, and all things are for God's glory.

GOD'S MISSIONARY PLAN FOR THE WORLD

How and when will "all Israel" be saved? The postmillennial view would be that sometime in the future there will be a turning of Israel as a nation to Christ. Such a wonderful event would be the occasion of the triumph of the Gospel throughout the world. Then would begin the period of universal peace and prevailing righteousness which would endure for a thousand years, either literally a thousand years or a long period. Following that period Christ will return for judgment, and the new heavens and the new earth will follow. This is the postmillennial plan. There are so many difficulties attending this interpretation of Scripture that scholars today have largely abandoned it in favor of what is called the amillennial view. That is the view that there will be no future millennium. But "all Israel" must be saved in the future.

Some amillenarians believe that this conversion of Israel will occur at the coming of Christ. This great event of Israel's turning to the Gospel must occur before the return of Christ, or at the coming of Christ. The statement in Revelation 1:7 would suggest that when Christ returns the tribes of Israel will mourn: "Behold, he is coming with the clouds, and every eye will see him, even those who pierced him, and all tribes of the earth will wail on account of him. Even so. Amen." This is also suggested in the description of the time of Jacob's trouble, Jeremiah 30; and the prophecies in Zechariah 12:10 to 13:6 indicate that Israel will be unbelieving at the time of the Lord's return. The brothers of Joseph when they were revealed to him were in great sorrow. There was not joy at the revelation, because they had rejected him. This would seem to be a real picture of God's people Israel at the coming of the Lord.

If that is so, it will mean that they will be converted when they look on Him whom they pierced. This does not necessarily mean that every individual Jew will be saved, but that Israel nationally, many gathered back to Palestine who pass through great tribulation, will accept their Messiah. Leading amillenarians such as Dr. E. H. Hamilton, take the view that this is what will happen. Then according to the amillennial view, Israel will instantly be raptured along with other believers, and be joined to the Body of Christ. That is, they will instantly cease to be Israel when they are saved.

It would seem that this conclusion is contrary to the whole tenor of Scripture. Israel was never an end in itself, but always a means to an end. Abraham was chosen from the beginning to be a blessing to all the nations of the earth. At the first coming of Christ, when Israel rejected the Messiah, a remnant accepted Him, and through this remnant blessing came to all the nations of the earth. But at the Second

Coming of Christ, when "all Israel" accepts Christ, there will flow correspondingly greater blessing to all nations of the earth. If that is true, it is another evidence of the premillennial view. The kingdom is then restored to Israel. This does not mean that Israel will be exalted as a proud nation over all other nations. It means that Israel will have the privilege of carrying out the original plan of God to make them a blessing to all nations of the earth; for the gifts and calling of God are not repented of.

The view of many Christians that this glorious purpose of God was completely fulfilled when the believing remnant of Israel were formed into the Church of Christ and became the evangelists for all the nations of the world, does not take account of definite Bible prophecies in both the Old Testament and in the New; nor does it take account of the facts of history. If that view were correct, there is no reason for the continuance of the Jews, scattered among all nations. Nor would there be any reason for their continued persecution. About the only reason that has been advanced is that God is preserving them in order to show that His Word is true, and that "all Israel will be saved." This ignores the fact that Israel's salvation is always for the purpose of blessing other nations. So far as the salvation of the individuals is concerned, this could take place quite as well if they had no connection with the nation of Israel.

Dr. William J. Erdman, and doubtless others, has summed up all Bible prophecy in these four great movements:

1. The Sin and Judgment of Israel.
2. The Sin and Judgment of the Nations.
3. The Repentance and Restoration of Israel.
4. The Repentance and Blessing of the Nations.

These great movements have been carried out in cycles, and

carried out partially again and again. At the close of the Old Testament story there was a culmination of the sin of Israel, resulting in the destruction of the temple and the judgment of the seventy years of captivity. At the end of seventy years there was the judgment upon Babylon—the world empire, for her sin. There was the repentance and restoration of a remnant of Israel, who returned to Jerusalem and built the temple. Out from this remnant there came the Messiah.

In the New Testament period, there was the sin of Israel in rejecting her Messiah, first when they crucified Him, and then when they rejected the risen Saviour. There followed the destruction of the temple and not seventy years of captivity, but nineteen hundred years of dispersion among the nations, suffering terrific tribulation. This long period will climax in the greatest of all the tribulations that Israel has had. But from that will come the final repentance and restoration of Israel as a whole. This will be followed by the repentance and blessing of the nations, who will as nations acknowledge Israel's Messiah.

At the beginning of this New Testament period there was the repentance and restoration of a remnant of Israel. The rejection of Messiah was not complete. Through this remnant, there have followed the blessings of this present Gospel age. What then will it be when Israel as a whole acknowledge Christ? Paul expresses it, "Life from the dead."

This, then, is God's marvelous missionary plan for the world. From the beginning it has been the Jew first, and also the Gentile. This does not mean that the Church age is a parenthesis. As a matter of fact, the Mosaic period was the parenthesis. The law was "It was added because of transgressions, until the offspring should come." The Lord's plan is a progressive, glorious plan through the various dispensations. But always salvation is by grace through faith. And always this plan is the Jew first, and also the Gentile.

After our Lord had spoken to the disciples during the space of forty days concerning the kingdom of God, they asked Him a question, "Lord, will you at this time restore the kingdom to Israel?" (Acts 1:6). It has been judged by some that this question sprang out of their ignorance, and out of their misconception of the new spiritual dispensation. Presumably, they had the wrong Judaistic idea of the restoring of the kingdom to Israel. But this view surely is not gathered from the answer of our Lord. He said, "It is not for you to know times or seasons that the Father has fixed by his own authority. But you will receive power when the Holy Spirit has come upon you, and you will be my witnesses in Jerusalem and in all Judea and Samaria, and to the end of the earth" (Acts 1:7-8).

Since the question of the disciples does not fit in with the interpretation that God has no further plan for Israel, it is natural to brush aside the force of the question by saying it was due to their ignorance. But why should the disciples ask about "restoring the kingdom to Israel"? It must have had some connection with the fact that our Lord definitely said that the kingdom of God was to be taken away from Israel (Matt. 21:43). Where did they get the idea that it would be restored? If it was a false idea, does it not seem strange that their question should follow upon the statement that the Lord had been speaking to them of things concerning the kingdom of God? If His speaking about the kingdom was according to this view that Israel as a nation had no more to do with it, why should that instruction of His bring forth such a question? Why would they not ask Him whether or not the kingdom was to be restored to Israel?

Our Lord's answer to their question would seem to imply that the kingdom was to be restored to Israel. The natural interpretation is that the disciples knew that this was true, and our Lord takes for granted that they knew. He virtually says, "This is not the time, and it is not for you to be concerned about that, but concerned about this other thing." If this is not what the Lord meant, then His words not only avoided answering their question, but were in danger of giving the wrong impression. And yet our Lord on another occasion said, "If it were not so, I would have told you." He never hesitated to change their wrong views. Would He avoid doing so regarding such an important matter? The normal, natural understanding of this question and answer is that the kingdom is to be restored to Israel, but not until the Gospel has been taken by the Church to the uttermost part of the earth.

This, then, is the challenge of God's missionary plan to us. We have received power for just one purpose—to be witnesses. The goal of that witness is the uttermost part. This Great Commission in Acts 1:8 is not simply a command. It is also a prophecy. The Gospel will go in this age, by the power of the Holy Spirit, through the Church, to the uttermost part of the earth. To suppose that some remnant of Israel after the Church is taken away will complete this witness, is to bring confusion again into the missionary plan of God. The Holy Spirit was sent for a definite purpose. He will be able to say to the Father and to the Son, "I have finished the work which you gave me to do." That work obviously is not the conversion of the world. Very obviously also it is not to get all the nations to acknowledge Christ officially as Saviour and Lord. The Old Testament speaks of a nation being born in a day. That will probably be the nation of Israel, when Christ comes. In any case, the first nation that will repent and be restored will be the nation of Israel. Then in God's order, repentance and blessing of the Gentile nations will follow.

One of the grand prophecies of the Old Testament is that all nations will bow before Him: "May he have dominion from sea to sea, and from the River to the ends of the earth…May all kings fall down before him, all nations serve him" (Ps. 72:8-11). Again, "All the nations you have made shall come and worship before you, O Lord, and shall glorify your name" (Ps. 86:9). Again, "All the ends of the earth shall remember and turn to the LORD, and all the families of the nations shall worship before you. For kingship belongs to the Lord, and he rules over the nations" (Ps. 22:27-28).

When is this to take place? According to the amillennial view it cannot take place in this present age. It must then take place in the new heavens and the new earth. But who will say that the resurrected saints, who presumably will occupy the new heavens and the new earth, fulfill this prophecy of all the nations of the earth bowing down before Christ? is there not needed the millennial reign of Christ when these nations on earth shall bow before Him?

There is the other sure prophecy that the nations on earth shall beat their swords into plowshares, their spears into pruning hooks. All of the weapons of war will be turned into instruments of peace. When will that take place? According to the amillennial view it cannot take place in this age. It must then take place in the new heavens and in the new earth. But who will say that this is a fulfillment of the prophecy? Certainly the risen saints who are occupying the new heavens and the new earth will not have any swords to beat into plowshares. They say that this is simply a figurative expression of the fact that there will be peace on earth. But it would seem natural that the very nations that have used the instruments of war would change them into the instruments of peace. This will require an age of universal peace and prevailing righteousness.

Many thoughtful and devoted Bible students have turned from the belief in Christ's premillennial coming because it has been associated with views about Israel and the Church which they cannot accept as being Scriptural. It is well, therefore, to view this question from the standpoint of what are the essential truths of the premillennial position, as over against the postmillennial and amillennial explanations. We may reject the view that all the prophecies of the Old Testament are fulfilled, or will be fulfilled, through the Church in this present age. But also, we may reject the view that none of the prophecies of the Old Testament concerning Israel are fulfilled in this present age. We can take the view that many of the prophecies are gloriously fulfilled, or are beginning to be fulfilled in this present age, while other prophecies such as the prophecy of the ultimate return of Israel to Palestine, and the return of Israel to the Lord, await fulfillment at the Second Coming of Christ. Indeed, the Old Testament prophecies as a whole set forth, as Peter says, "the sufferings of Christ and the subsequent glories" (1 Pet. 1:11).

Again and again the prophecy of the first and second coming of Christ is put together in the Old Testament, and the things that happened in the first coming and the second coming are put together as though they were one glorious event. And so in looking forward to the Second Coming of Christ the prophecies often speak of events at the beginning of the thousand years and at the end of the thousand years as though they occurred at the same time.

Let us close this discussion of God's missionary plan as set forth in Romans 9 to 11, by quoting one of the remarkable prophecies concerning Israel in Hosea 3:4-5: "For the children of Israel shall dwell many days without king or prince, without sacrifice or pillar, without ephod or household gods. Afterward the children of Israel shall return and seek the Lord their God, and David their king, and they shall come in fear to the LORD and to his goodness in the latter days." Israel today is abiding without her true King, the Lord Jesus, and also without any earthly prince. She is without the true sacrifice, having rejected Calvary, hut she is also without any heathen "pillar," a false sacrifice. She is without the ephod, the revelation of God through the Holy Spirit; but also, she has not accepted the teraphim, or the heathen oracles. But the children of Israel shall return and seek the Lord their God and David their king. David their king is, of course, the Lord Jesus Christ. They will come with fear to the Lord and to His goodness in the latter days.

When will those last days come about? Certainly they have not yet come, but that God has a future purpose for Israel as a nation should be one of the clearest interpretations of Scripture, and one of the plainest facts of history. And when they come to Christ it will be with the same purpose that God chose them in the beginning, to be a blessing to all the nations.

Preparation for Lesson 11

Reading Lesson: Romans 12 - 13

A. *The Surrendered Life* (chapter 12)

1. What must precede the surrendered life? What is the relation of the twelfth chapter of Romans to what goes before? Note especially 11:33-36.

2. What is meant by "spiritual service" in verse 1? What is meant by the "good and perfect and acceptable will of God"?

3. What do the many members in one body (verses 3 to 8) teach concerning the surrendered life? In what other chapters of tile Bible is the Body of Christ specially considered?

4. Count the commands given in Romans 12.

5. Do verses 5 to 21 suggest that, after all, works have a good deal to do with Christian living? What is the relation of these verses to the message of salvation?

B. *The Christian and the State in This Present Age* (chapter 13)

6. What two things are governments commissioned to do? Why should Christians support them in this? What is the relation of these verses to the message of salvation by grace?

7. What should be a Christian's attitude toward war? Does this passage give light upon it?

8. Should the Church take part in politics? What should the attitude of a Christian be toward prohibition and Sunday laws?

9. What does Paul mean by salvation being nearer than when they first believed? What does he call this present age? When will it end?

Lesson 11

Exhortation to True Christian Living

Romans 12:1–15:13

THE GREAT APPEAL FOR THE YIELDED LIFE—12:1-2

The riches and the glories of the grace of God have been set forth. What is our response? God has given Himself to us in Christ. Shall we give the one sacrifice that is well pleasing, the sacrifice of ourselves, to serve Him in the Spirit, living out in daily life the good, and acceptable, and perfect will of God?

Note the words, "I appeal to you therefore, brothers, by the mercies of God." The appeal to surrender to Christ is made on the basis of the glorious plan of salvation set forth in the first eleven chapters of Romans. He says to present, or yield, or surrender our bodies—that is, to yield ourselves while we are living in our bodies. This is called "a living sacrifice." The contrast is with the sacrifices of the old order, the animal sacrifices that were brought to Jewish altars. The sacrifice is holy, and it is well pleasing or delightful to God. It is our "spiritual service." The old version says, "reasonable service," and it surely is the reasonable or the logical thing to do, to yield ourselves to Christ, after all He has done for us. However, the sense of the original is somewhat different from this. He is speaking of the spiritual worship of the new order, as over against the outward, carnal worship of the old order.

The New Testament speaks of spiritual sacrifices (I Pet. 2:5). When we give money it is a spiritual sacrifice, well pleasing to Him (Phil.

4:18). When we sing praise, it is the fruit of lips, giving sacrifice to God (Heb. 13:15). And here is the central sacrifice in our spiritual worship, the giving of ourselves. When we do that, we prove the will of God in our lives. He says three things about the will of God. It is good, the very best thing that immeasurable love and infinite power can plan for the loved one; it is well pleasing—it pleases God: we may "walk in a manner worthy of the Lord, fully pleasing to him" (Col. 1:10); it is perfect, the final word for us, and this sure guidance we may have step by step along the pathway of the present life (cf. Eph. 4:1).

THE WORKING OUT OF THE YIELDED LIFE—12:3-21

1. OUR INDIVIDUAL SPIRITUAL GIFTS—12:3-8

Our Christian living and service are to be in the power of the Spirit. Each has his own "gift." "Each according to the measure of faith that God has assigned." This verse has been used to teach that every man who is born is given "a measure of faith." If he improves that faith, he is saved. If not, he is lost. But this does not refer to faith for salvation. He is speaking to believers who already have been born of the Spirit, and have been baptized by the Spirit into the Body of Christ.

Again, these words "a measure of faith" have given rise to a striking and much-used phrase "the analogy of faith." All teachings are to conform to what is called "the analogy of faith," gathered from the message of the whole Bible. This is true, but it is not what Paul is speaking about here. He is speaking about the members of the Body of Christ, and the gifts that each member has. There are two other chapters that set forth in a special way this wonderful message of the one Body in Christ, and its many members, the fourth of Ephesians and the twelfth of Second Corinthians. Many have used the twelfth chapter of Second Corinthians to define the "gifts of the Spirit" as extraordinary gifts for special things, such as speaking in tongues, and prophesying. But here in the twelfth of Romans it is made evident that all activities of the Christian are to be in the power of the Spirit. Such commonplace things as the giving of money, and showing mercy, are included along with "prophesying" or "teaching."

Thus the thought of serving "according to the measure of faith" means that if we go beyond that gift of the Spirit, we are serving in the energy of the flesh. How often a preacher in his earnest exhortation before a congregation may get so emotionally wrought up that much of the exhortation is in the energy of the flesh. He has not been exhorting "according to the proportion of faith."

All recognize that it requires the power of the Spirit to prophesy. Here the word signifies not foretelling events, but preaching the truth. We also need the power of the Spirit for ministry in the Church of Christ, and for teaching and exhorting. The work of a deacon or a trustee needs the guidance of the Spirit. To show mercy and hospitality require the presence and the power of the Spirit. We cannot even give money except in the Spirit, if we are really giving. We are to give with singleness of heart as unto the Lord. The fruit of the Spirit is the same for all Christians, although there are differences of degree in the manifestation of that fruit. But the gifts of the Spirit are different for each Christian, even as one member in the body differs from another.

2. THE LAW OF LOVE IN ALL RELATIONSHIPS—12:9-21

"Abhor what is evil; hold fast to what is good." This is the Christian way of dealing with temptation to evil— keep far away from the border line, and have a passion for that which is holy. "Overcome evil with good." That is the Christian way of dealing with evil done against us. As God's grace abounded where sin abounded, so does His grace through us abound. Thus are we not merely conquerors of evil, but "more than conquerors."

There are in the twelfth chapter of Romans about forty distinct commandments, if each one be counted separately. Romans is a message on grace abounding. What is the relation between that salvation by grace and these commandments? Are these New Testament commandments different from "the law"? Paul has been insistent that we are saved by grace, through faith, apart from works. Where, then, do these works come in? It is evidence of the attack of Satan against all Christian truth that there should be in the minds of Christians such confusion over the question of relationship between grace and law. Part of the confusion is due to the fact that the word "law" is used in the New Testament with at least ten different meanings or different emphases. For example, the first five books of the Old Testament are called "the law" (Luke 24:44). Again, the "law" may refer to the Old Testament (John 10:34). We have seen that "law" is used in the sense of the principle, as "the law of the Spirit of life." Then the word "law" may be used as equivalent to the Word: "O how love I Your law, it is my meditation all the day." One of the most frequent uses of the word "law" is to designate the Mosaic law, the whole system under which Israel was from Sinai to the Cross of Christ. Another frequent use of the word "law" is to designate God's moral law. This moral law is the same in all dispensations; it is included in the Mosaic law, and is also an expression of God's will in the Gospel age. The word "law" in its original significance has the thought of "teaching." These commandments in the twelfth chapter of Romans are an expression of God's will for the Christian, and of course, God's will for every man. It was said of our Lord that He delighted to do God's will: "Your law is within my heart" (Ps. 40:8; Heb. 10:7). Here we have the meaning of "law" as an expression of the will of God.

The plain and simple teaching of God's Word is that faith without works is dead. That is, if a man really has faith, it will be evidenced by his works. What are those good works? They are nothing other than living the life in accordance with God's will. Paul has made it evident that no man is justified or declared righteous by the works of the law. Faith excludes all works. But true faith is evidenced by works. And so works without faith are dead works. Faith without works is dead faith. That is, it is not real faith. Why should there be any confusion here?

Some, in the eager desire to separate the Christian from everything connected with "law," teach that Christians need "instruction," which they consider is different from law. When God says, "See that no one repays anyone evil for evil," or, "Love your enemies and pray for those who persecute you," it is suggested that these statements contain instruction, and are not law. The confusion here comes from thinking of "law" in only one sense, namely, in the sense of a command that must be obeyed on the penalty of death. But we are not under the condemnation of the law. We are under grace. This does not mean that we are excused from observing God's righteous commandments. Grace is not excusing us from walking in the will of God, but it is God's way of enabling us to walk in His will. But what is His will? This must be expressed to us by His commandments. God does not give advice. He does not say that He would be pleased if a man out of the love of his heart for the Lord should tell the truth. He says, "Do not lie to one another." He says, "You shall not commit adultery." These moral commands expressed in the Ten Commandments are binding in the New

Testament dispensation as well as in the Old.

Some suggest that when a man is indwelt by the Spirit of God, he naturally will love his neighbor, he naturally will refrain from murder and adultery. In this sense they say he does not need the law. But this is based on a fallacy. We need the revelation of God's will as to what is good. We are born into a human race that has had the revelation of God's law for thousands of years. There are some things that we instinctively regard as right or wrong, which we have accepted as the truth of God. But Christians do not instinctively do what is right because the Holy Spirit is dwelling within them. The Holy Spirit works always in connection with the Word of God, and we need the revelation of God as to what is right. The Holy Spirit gives power to walk in that way, but He does it through our knowledge of the Word, and through the gifts that God has given which enable us to understand the Word. One is the gift of our intelligence. God must deal with infants and those with special needs in a way that is different from those who have their intelligence, and can understand these commands. Just because we are "under grace," we are the more eager to learn what the commandments of God are. Our Lord Himself distinctly says, "Whoever has my commandments and keeps them, he it is who loves me." (John 14:21). Love is not a soft sentimental feeling that we have concerning our Lord. Love is proved by obedience, and for obedience we must have commands. One of our greatest needs today among Christian young people is to live by ethical standards based in God's commands.

There is one expression in the old version, "not slothful in business" (12:11), which is changed in the Revised Version to something entirely different: "in diligence not slothful." It is true that Christians ought not to be slothful in business, but Paul is here speaking of spiritual things, and not of secular business. As a matter of fact, some of the greatest scoundrels in the world are not slothful in business. Indeed, those who are crooked in business are usually very diligent. In this case also the children of the world are for their own generation wiser than the children of light. What Paul says here goes much deeper. He means that in our spiritual activities we should have great diligence and not be slothful, but rather, "fervent in spirit," serving the Lord, that is, doing all things as unto Him. As we go on, we have great joy, because we rejoice in "the glory of God"; that makes us "patient in tribulation." But we are not left without a strong recourse in times of trouble and tribulation, for we continue steadfastly in prayer, showing great love to the saints, and also expressing love to the enemies. Indeed, the whole of the law as elsewhere is summed up in the one word "love." In relation to others we are to act so that they will know that we are "honorable." When he tells us, "If possible, so far as it depends on you, live peaceably with all." Paul is not saying that we should be at peace so far as our temper will hold out. He means that so far as we are able to control things, we should be at peace: "so far as it depends on you."

THE CHRISTIAN'S RELATION TO OTHERS— 13:1-14

1. HIS RELATION TO THE STATE—13:1.7

"Render to Caesar the things that are Caesar's," is our Lord's message which Paul passes on. He is speaking of human governments and human law in their legitimate place as servants of God in keeping order. The fact that the "powers that be" are ordained of God has no bearing on whether they exercise their powers rightly; our Lord told Pilate that he would have no power except it were given him from above; yet he was using that power to put to death the Son of God.

This statement concerning the powers that be was misinterpreted to support the doctrine of the "divine right of kings," which often resulted in the enslavement of great masses of people. It also has been used by good men to argue that the thirteen colonies never should have rebelled against England. But here Paul is not dealing with the right that people may have to change their government. He is dealing with government itself. In this age God has committed to the Gentile governments the ruling of the world. But Paul clearly defines in what sense he is speaking of rulers: "For rulers are not a terror to good conduct, but to bad. Would you have no fear of the one who is in authority? Then do what is good, and you will receive his approval, for he is God's servant for your good." He is not considering here the case of a government persecuting men because they do that which is good.

When Paul wrote these words one of the greatest monsters that ever sat on a throne was ruling in Rome, the Emperor Nero, who reigned from 54 to 68 AD. Yet he could say, "for he is God's servant for your good," not meaning Nero personally, but the government. Then Paul declares that the government has the duty to punish that which is evil, and in doing so, he uses the sword, that is, he employs the force of arms.

This passage has always been a difficulty, and indeed an unanswerable problem, to those who maintain that the use of force is always wrong. Others would agree that it is right for a police power to use force to keep down evil, but not right for a nation to go to war. We might agree that bandits in the United States must be suppressed at all cost. But must we say that if a nation like Germany or Japan should desire to conquer the United States and enslave its people, the government is doing an evil thing in using the Army and the Navy of the United States to prevent such an evil?

Perhaps the greatest confusion in the discussion of this question of war and peace arises from not seeing the clear distinction between the duty of governments to execute judgment and the duty of Christians to be governed by love in all of their attitudes. At the close of the twelfth chapter of Romans, we read, "Beloved, never avenge yourselves, but leave it to the wrath of God, for it is written, 'Vengeance is mine, I will repay, says the Lord'" (12:19). Then follows the strong word, "if your enemy is hungry, feed him; if he is thirsty, give him something to drink." Now in the thirteenth chapter Paul distinctly says that if the government bears the sword in punishing evildoers it is "for the authorities are ministers of God, attending to this very thing." Everyone can see that the judge who pronounces the death sentence is not a murderer. The members of the jury that declare that a man is guilty and vote for the death sentence are not committing murder. The executioner who turns on the electric switch to execute a criminal is not, thereby, a murderer. The reason is that it is the government that is trying and executing a man. But in back of the government is the law of God. There is no contradiction between this and loving our enemies. The judge may have to condemn his own son who stands before the bar, and he may do it with a broken heart.

There is much sentimental foolishness taught about the evils of war, and how war contradicts all of these commands of God to Christians with regard to loving their enemies. On the other hand, there is a fatal fallacy on the other side when officers tell their men that they must hate the enemy in order to be good fighters. Some of the greatest generals and officers and men have been most earnest Christians. American soldiers would be the first to show all kindness to wounded enemies when the battle is over.

This does not mean that war is not a terrible scourge. God's judgments are fearful things, but we will not accuse God of iniquity when He executes His strange work of judgment. A strict pacifism blots out moral distinctions. One of the heroes of the First World War, turning in bitter hatred toward everything connected with war, was explaining that one of the reasons Christian nations kept on with a method of war was because of the way they exalted their military heroes. He told of a father who took his son to see the statue of Wellington in a Canadian city, and explained to the boy what a great man the general was. This soldier's solution of the problem was that Wellington should be held up not as a great hero, but as one who brought grave injuries upon mankind because he took part in war. This would mean there is no difference between Wellington and Napoleon, no difference between Israel and the Canaanites, no difference between the United States and Japan, and ultimately this means that there is no difference between God and Satan. Otherwise, we must say that God can never put men to death, and He can never authorize governments to use force to put men to death.

If the use of force is always wrong, it would mean that it is utterly impossible for a Christian to live in this present world. Some would attempt to solve the problem by saying that a Christian should have nothing to do with government. He should not vote, nor hold public office. But in that event, he should not pay taxes either, for taxes constitute his share in what the government is doing. Here again Paul says that the government in collecting tribute is acting as a minister of God. It is the duty of Christians to pay taxes, and to pay taxes cheerfully, doing this as all things, unto the Lord. Thus the Bible will be found to be the most practical book in the world. The Christian message is not a theoretical thing. It takes account of things as they are. The miracle is that without compromise a Christian may "Pay to all what is owed to them: taxes to whom taxes are owed, revenue to whom revenue is owed, respect to whom respect is owed, honor to whom honor is owed." (13:7). The Christian, however, does not say, "Render to Caesar the things that are Caesar's." That is not his motto. His motto is: "Render to Caesar the things that are Caesar's, and to God the things that are God's."

2. HIS RELATION TO HIS NEIGHBOR—13:8-10

The message of the law of love runs throughout this section of Romans, and here the message climaxes in the wonderful summing up of love as the Christian way of keeping the law: "therefore love is the fulfilling of the law" (13:10).

This passage offers a difficulty to those who say that a Christian has nothing to do with fulfilling the law. Some would say that he is "under law to Christ," meaning that he must find God's requirement for him in the New Testament. But when Paul mentions the love of our neighbor as fulfilling the law, he quotes four of the Ten Commandments, those which have to do particularly with sins against our neighbor; and lest some literalist should say that these four are the only commandments incumbent on Christians, he adds: "any other commandment, are summed up in this word: 'You shall love your neighbor as yourself.'" This is an Old Testament commandment, and indeed is the summing up of the moral law, because it implies the first and great commandment, to love God with all the heart, and soul, and mind, and strength.

When we think of love in relation to God, and to our neighbor, the word may be used in three distinct senses. It may express God's standard for holy living. Again, it may express the motive or power that is in the heart, the source of holy actions. Again, it may express the attitude of faith toward God, the means by which we lay hold of God's power. The love of God is shed abroad in our hearts by the Holy Spirit. To live by the power of the Holy Spirit expresses a certain standard of living: "The fruit of the Spirit is love." How does love behave itself? Love expresses itself in love, joy, peace, patience, kindness, goodness, faithfulness, gentleness, self-control. Thus we have a standard for living. But the Holy Spirit is the power for living. If this distinction is kept in mind, we will not fall into the error of supposing that because we have the Holy Spirit in our hearts, that alone gives us the knowledge of what God's standards are. We must be told how love is to operate.

Paul's statement, "Owe no one anything, except to love each other," has been taken as a direct command from God that a Christian should never go into debt. He should never owe anyone anything. This interpretation certainly may lead to good results if it warns Christians against going into debt and obligating themselves for things that they are not sure that they can pay.

The context indicates that Paul is telling Christians to pay their debts: "Pay to all what is owed to them," whatever those dues may be. Therefore, his word, "Owe no man anything," is predicated on the thought that we are constantly owing things to other individuals and to our government, and we should pay the obligation. It would be impossible to live in this present world and never owe anything. Their interpretation of this injunction has led some to believe that it is wrong to take a mortgage on a property because they are going into debt. And yet if they pay rent to someone who owns the property, it may be costing them more than to own the property and have a mortgage. The fact is that the property stands for the mortgage, and the person to whom the money is owed is not injured by it, but rather benefited. At the same time there is a warning to Christians, and especially to

Christian institutions, not to go into debt. In any case, the message of this passage is far deeper than the matter of owing money. Paul is not concerned to say, "Owe no man anything." He wishes to press home in strong language the truth that the eternal debt of Christians is "to love one another." That is the debt that can never be avoided.

3. HIS RELATION TO THE WORLD AND THE FLESH—13:11-14

Now Paul sums up these exhortations of the Christian's relation to others in this present age by reminding them that the coming of the Lord Jesus Christ is drawing near. The normal way for a Christian to live is in the eager expectancy of the personal return of the Saviour. Paul says, "For salvation is nearer to us now than when we first believed" (13:11). What a statement is that, as nearly two thousand years have passed since Paul made the declaration! Paul did not mean that we were to struggle to get to the place of being saved. He is here speaking of the completion of our redemption. He makes another striking statement: "The night is far gone; the day is at hand." In another passage Paul speaks of this present age as "man's day" (1 Cor. 4:3). God calls it night! The glorious morning of God's day is at hand, the day of the completion of our salvation, spoken of in chapter eight. Christ is coming, as someone has said, not as the evening star at the close of the day, but as the bright and morning star, to usher in the new day, the day when the Prince of Peace will be crowned as the King of Righteousness. The emphasis is not on the number of years that may pass before that day is at hand. The emphasis is upon the distinction between the night and the day. And so the exhortation is: "So then let us cast off the works of darkness and put on the armor of light" (13:12).

Christians are to walk in this present age as children of the light, as those who are giving a present manifestation of what it will be when the day dawns. And so we are to have nothing to do with orgies and drunkenness, sexual immorality and sensuality, quarreling and jealousy. These things are of the flesh. Then there is a glorious summing up of the whole appeal of the Gospel: "But put on the Lord Jesus Christ, and make no provision for the flesh, to gratify its desires" (13:14).

Preparation for Lesson 12

Reading Lesson: Romans 14:1–16:27

A. *Judging Doubtful Things and Judging One Another* (14:1–15:13)

1. Notice that Paul gives the same principle for dealing with the matter of judging as he does for guiding our relation to the State and to others.

2. What "questionable things" troubled these Roman Christians? What are some of the questionable things that trouble Christians today?

3. How is Christ given as an example? How does the great Jew and Gentile question come up again?

B. *The Closing Personal Messages* (15:14 –16:27)

1. Note the subjects mentioned in the opening personal messages that are taken up again as Paul closes the letter.

2. Note Paul's great missionary ambition.

3. Note the significance of the names in chapter 16, and the comments accompanying them.

4. What is the meaning of the promise in 16:20?

5. Note the summing up of the message in the doxology.

6. What has impressed you most about this letter to the Romans?

Lesson 12

Closing Messages and Greeting

JUDGING DOUBTFUL THINGS, JUDGING ONE ANOTHER
—14:1–15:13

Paul now turns to practical problems facing these Christians in their relation to one another. They are facing questions of ceremonies, problems raised by the relation between Jewish Christians and Gentile Christians, and the relation of all Christians to the heathen round about them. In giving them God's will concerning these matters, Paul is establishing great principles that are to govern Christians today in judging doubtful things, and judging one another, even though we do not face just the problems that they faced.

Here again, in solving every problem, the law of love is at the center. The Christian is called in liberty, and is not bound by laws of ritual, but he is to walk by faith. Yet the highest law is love, and those weak in knowledge and faith should be received and helped. There is a special need that Jews and Gentiles should receive one another, and rejoice together in their one Lord. Some of these Hebrew Christians at Rome were judging their stronger brethren who had faith to eat all things, and some of the stronger Christians were putting down the weaker Christians, glorying in their own clearer knowledge. "Knowledge puffs up, but love builds up" (1 Cor. 8:1-13). In everything, the aim of love is to build up our brother, and not to please ourselves. In this, as in all things, Christ Himself is our example, as He is our enabling power to walk even as He walked.

In the matter of judging, our first concern should be to judge ourselves and our own conduct that we may not put a stumbling block or an occasion of falling in a brother's way. We are not to have a judging spirit, and then we shall be in a position to "judge righteous judgment." We are to remember the future day when all Christians are to stand before the judgment seat of Christ, to receive our praise of God or our blame from God. For each one of us must give account to God for the way he has used the wonderful gifts of His grace (2 Cor. 5:10; Col. 3:24-25).

Paul deals with the question of eating, and of observing days. "One person esteems one day as better than another, while another esteems all days alike" (14:5). The word "alike" does not appear in the original. This verse is interpreted by many as referring to the Lord's Day, and that we are at liberty to regard the Lord's Day as a sacred day or not to regard it so.

If this is what the passage meant, it would indeed be a serious matter. It would mean that the setting apart of the first day of the week as the Lord's Day is entirely an individual, optional matter. What would be the practical result of such a view? One of the most precious gifts of God to His Church and to the world is the gift of the Lord's Day. The blessing of God upon the nations can almost be judged by the measure in which this day is honored. What a priceless privilege we have in America, that nearly all business stops, and all the churches are opened, so that we may worship on the first day of the week. How did it come about? Did it come about because Christians out of their love for the Lord decided that it would be a good thing to remember the day of His resurrection? Has the Lord's Day no connection with the Old Testament Sabbath? Have the Ten Commandments of the old dispensation been changed to nine commandments in the New? There are those that tell us that Christians have nothing whatever to do with the fourth commandment, nor with the Sabbath Day. We keep the first day of the week apart from any command of God. This means that one of the greatest needs that human beings have, that is, one day in seven for the rest and for the special worship of God, is an institution that man himself has proposed to God. We have indeed the example of the Old Testament, and we gather from that example that it might be a good thing for us in this dispensation to honor God by keeping the first day of the week.

All of this reasoning is quite contrary to the Scripture, and is quite contrary to the interpretation that the Church has given from the very beginning. The moral law of God, based on the nature of God and the nature of man, began in the garden of Eden. It entered unchanged into the Mosaic law. When Christ died and rose again, and the Mosaic system was forever done, the moral law entered unchanged into the new dispensation, even as God's plan of salvation by grace entered unchanged.

It is certainly true that there are different dispensations, in which God varies His dealing with men. But there are two essential points at which God has never varied His dealings with men. Salvation by grace through faith, founded on the righteousness of Christ and His precious blood, has been unchanged throughout all dispensations. God has never had more than one way of getting into favor with God. But just as salvation by grace through faith is unchanged, so are God's moral standards unchanged in all dispensations. Indeed, that moral standard of absolute obedience to God, that righteousness which God must require of all His creatures, is inseparably linked with God's plan of redemption. He must provide Christ as our righteousness. He must pay the penalty for that broken law. This is the glad news. Then, set free from the curse of the law, that law which is an expression of the will of God, becomes to us our great delight.

To observe the Lord's Day in a legalistic fashion would be to make it a burden and a bondage. But to observe this day as the Lord's Day, governing our conduct in a special way, separated from the other days of the week, this will indeed be love fulfilling the law. We are not bound by Old Testament regulations as to what is fitting on the seventh day of the week, and what is not fitting. We are bound by the sanction of God's law to set this day aside as a day of rest and worship.

Our Lord in His matchless way summed up the truth of the Sabbath by saying two things: "The Sabbath was made for man, not man for the Sabbath." And "So the Son of Man is lord even of the Sabbath" (Mark 2:27-28).

This word of Christ's as other words of Scripture, has been twisted into a meaning that contradicts the very thing He was saying. The Sabbath was made for man, we argue, and therefore, man is the one to determine what is wise for him to do or to leave undone on the Sabbath. But man, who is not capable of telling what is good for him in other ways, is certainly not the one to determine what is good for him on the Sabbath Day. The purpose of the Sabbath Day is to provide the rest and worship that men need. Therefore, if a man, misinterpreting the Lord's Word, spends the day in recreation, in his own pleasure, in going to his office for business, in traveling here and there to carry out his own plans—is he proving that the day was made for man? No, he is contradicting that very truth. He is putting aside the benefits that God planned when He ordained and commanded that one day in seven should be set apart as holy unto Him. Note also that the Sabbath was made for man, not for the Jew only.

CLOSING PERSONAL MESSAGES AND GREETINGS— ROMANS 15:14–16:27

There appears to be no break at the fourteenth verse, which begins with "and." Yet it is evident that from 15:14 on the letter deals with Paul's personal relation to the Romans as the Apostle to the Gentiles, discusses the reason for writing them, his purpose to visit them, and in a remarkable manner returns to all the subjects of the opening messages in the first chapter, supplementing what he has said, and completing it. In the first chapter he has said: "For I long to see you, that I may impart to you some spiritual gift to strengthen you" (1:11). In the majestic closing doxology he writes: "Now to him who is able to strengthen you according to my gospel and the preaching of Jesus Christ."

PAUL'S MISSIONARY "AMBITION"—15:14-21

Paul's commission as Apostle to the Gentiles has been attested by the marvelous success of his ministry through the power of the Spirit. Here he gives his great missionary "ambition," an ambition that should give the key for the missionary motive and purpose of the Church of Christ today. This word which is translated in the Revised Version "making it my aim" and in the old version "so have I strived," occurs only three times in the New Testament. Twice Paul uses it as a personal testimony of his own, and in doing so he gives the two ambitions that should control the life of every Christian. In 2 Corinthians 5:9 he writes: "So whether we are at home or away, we make it our aim to please him." As Paul looks forward to the great judgment seat of Christ, he desires to be well pleasing to the Lord at that time. Therefore, his great ambition in his present living is to be well pleasing to Christ now. The parallel expressed in Romans 15 is the carrying out of that other desire to be well pleasing unto Christ. He makes it his ambition "preach the gospel, not where Christ has already been named, lest I build on someone else's foundation; but, as it is written, "Those who have never been told of him will see, and those who have never heard will understand."

Our Lord Jesus gave one Great Commission to the Church. He did not give two commissions, but just one. That was the commission to take the Gospel to every creature. In proportion as the Church of Christ as a whole, and the various "denominations" of churches, and the individual Christians have been true to this commission of Christ, to that extent there has come great spiritual blessing. Our Lord Jesus had one great passion expressed in this commission, set forth in each of the four Gospels, and in Acts 1:8. Therefore, Paul with his desire to be well pleasing to Christ, must be consumed with this one great passion, to make Christ known. This, Paul points out, is the goal of Old Testament prophecy, and also of New Testament prophecy. In Acts 1:8 when our Lord told the disciples that they should receive power, the Holy Spirit coming upon them, it was that they should be witnesses to the uttermost part of the earth. This is not a command only, it is a prophecy. The Gospel will go to the uttermost part of the earth. The Holy Spirit will finish that for which He was sent to do. Even as our Lord said: "I glorified you on earth, having accomplished the work that you gave me to do." so the Holy Spirit will say, to the Father, and to the Son: "I glorified you on earth, having accomplished the work that you gave me to do." It is not some future group of people separate from the Church who are to finish Christ's Commission in this age. The Holy Spirit was sent to the Church, and while it is clearly predicted that there will be a great apostasy, and the organized Church as a whole will fail Christ, even as Israel as a nation failed Him, yet the faithful believing remnant, in the power of the Spirit, will carry the Gospel to the uttermost part of the earth.

There are those who say that Paul actually completed this work of taking the Gospel to the uttermost part of the earth. This is based on Colossians 1:23: "if indeed you continue in the faith, stable and steadfast, not shifting from the hope of the gospel that you heard, which has been proclaimed in all creation under heaven, and of which I, Paul, became a minister." If it is true that these prophecies refer to the first generation, then the expression "uttermost part of the earth" referred to the then known earth, and referred to the comparatively small world of Paul's day. However, there is no need to interpret this passage as declaring that the Gospel had gone to all the earth. The emphasis is that the Gospel they had is the same Gospel that had gone throughout the world, using the expression "all creation" in a general sense. In any case, this view that the Gospel did go to the uttermost part in Paul's day is a testimony to the clear revelation of God's Word that the Gospel must go to the uttermost part of the earth before the return of our Lord.

Thus, today we have as the most tremendous of all the signs that point toward the coming of the Lord, the mighty missionary movements that give promise of finishing the Great Commission in our generation. One of the great purposes in the permission of the World War was God's turning and overturning of the nations, and opening the way for the Gospel to go to every tribe that has not yet heard.

The great shame of the American Church, and of all churches, and the great shame of our seminaries and training institutions is the fact that the bulk of the money, and of the men and women, has been used for the local work, and a very small proportion toward the carrying out of the one great passion of our Lord. On the other hand, we see the blessing of God upon the nations that have been foremost in carrying out the Great Commission. Many churches are catching the vision of giving at least fifty percent of all of their money toward foreign missions, and some training institutions are aiming to send fifty percent of their young men and women to make Christ known where His Name has never been named. This will not be to the neglect of the great need at home, but to an outpouring of blessing that there will not be room to receive it.

PAUL'S PURPOSE OF VISITING THEM—15:22-29

As Paul explains his plans to go to Spain and visit them on the way he finds occasion again to refer to the spiritual relation of Jew and Gentile, and to add another of those priceless gems as found in these closing messages: "I know that when I come to you I will come in the fullness of the blessing of Christ;" and if they get the real message of this letter, they will receive Paul in the fullness. We are not sure that Paul ever got to Spain, but there is no proof that he did not. We are reminded that the Acts and the Epistles of the New Testament are not intended to give a full account of the labors of Paul and other apostles. Only those things are included which are necessary to the revelation.

Paul here has occasion also to present the spiritual meaning of giving money. The Gentiles have received spiritual things from the Jews and it was right that they should minister unto them of carnal things. There were many "poor among the saints that are at Jerusalem" because of their loyalty to Christ, and their separation from the other Jews.

HIS REQUEST FOR THEIR PRAYERS—15:30-33

They are to strive together with Paul in their prayers! What a privilege! Are we sharing in the triumphs of our missionaries today through our striving in prayer? Notice the precious expression "By the love of the Spirit." Paul never forgets the Father, and the Son, and the Spirit. He has been telling them in Romans that all things that they do are to be done by the Holy Spirit. He has told them of the love of God which has been shed abroad in our hearts by the Holy Spirit. He is reminding them that the Holy Spirit is the Spirit of love. When Christians are conscious of the love of the Spirit, that will make our love go out to our fellow believers and especially to those who are in the forefront of the battle, that they might be delivered from all the powers of darkness that are against them. The portion of the Christian worker is opposition and tribulation, but there is also "joy through the will of God," and "rest," and fellowship with other believers, and in the presence of "the God of peace."

PERSONAL SALUTATIONS—16:1–16:24

1. COMMENDING PHOEBE, WHO CARRIES THE LETTER— 16:1-2

Here is this letter which has been acclaimed even by unbeliev ers as the greatest document ever penned by a human being, and it is carried by Phoebe, a faithful Christian who has helped many and who has helped Paul. Thus, we see the glory and greatness of God's salvation linked with all of the ordinary affairs of life. Paul asks them to receive Phoebe, and to assist her in the business that she has. This is true Christian helpfulness to those who have been thoughtful to others.

2. SALUTING MANY THAT ARE KNOWN TO PAUL—16:3-16

Do not pass over this section as a mere list of names. What a goodly fellowship this is! And is it not a suggestion of the praise our Lord will give each one of His brethren, recognizing and appreciating every good thing? How rich in meaning are some of these incidental comments, among them this: "they were in Christ before me." What a reality in those words "in Christ," one of the expressions that runs through all of Paul's writings and gives the key to his Gospel.

There are twenty-six names that are mentioned, and in addition to these there is the sister, and the mother, the household, the Church that is in their house, the brethren or the saints that are with them.

3. WARNING AGAINST THOSE CAUSING STUMBLING— 16:17-20

In every church there are enemies within as well as without. Satan's great masterpiece is to cause "division." This, of course, does not refer to divisions that come because those who are faithful to God's Word protest against those who are denying God's Word. The divisions and occasions of stumbling he speaks of are "contrary the doctrine that you have been taught." Thus is "doctrine," or "teaching," linked always with the actual living out of the truth in life. But in spite of these difficulties in the Church, Paul is rejoicing in their obedience, and we should ever rejoice in the good things that are in the Church, and also should be "wise as to what is good and innocent as to what is evil." Ours is not a complicated matter to understand all of the meaning of evil. Our part is to center on Christ and following His will.

Again this paragraph closes with another of those exceeding great and precious promises: "The grace of our Lord Jesus Christ be with you" (16:20). This takes us back to the Protevangelium, the first prophecy of Christ in the Bible, in Genesis 3:15. The seed of the woman, our Lord Jesus Christ, will bruise the head of the serpent, and the Lord's people are to be associated with Him in this defeat of Satan. It is always "shortly" for the Church of Christ in every generation. The great climax of this will come when our Lord Jesus returns. Again, there is one of the several doxologies found in the closing section of Romans: "The grace of our Lord Jesus Christ be with you." And yet Paul had a further word.

4. GREETINGS FROM COMPANIONS OF PAUL, INCLUDING TERTIUS WHO WRITES THE LETTER—16:21-24

Eight more names are added of those who join with Paul in sending greetings to the brethren at Rome. A higher critic may here say that the whole of Romans is not the work of Paul, because he allows his secretary or amanuensis (one employed to write from dictation or to copy manuscript) to insert one sentence: "I Tertius, who write the epistle, salute you in the Lord." Then there is Gaius, Paul's host, probably the one who had the distinction of being baptized by Paul's own hands, and also the one to whom John wrote his third Epistle.

CLOSING OUTBURST OF PRAISE TO THE GOD OF ALL GRACE—16:25-27

A fitting climax to this most wonderful of all letters is the glorious ascription of praise to God our Saviour. Again, the message of the epistle is summed up, "my Gospel," the mystery kept in silence through the ages, and now made known to all the nations that they may obey God by believing in Jesus Christ. Some would say that this "mystery" was not revealed by Paul until later in his life, and given through Ephesians and Colossians. But there is one Gospel from Genesis 3:15 through to the end of Revelation. And in this letter we have a complete setting forth of the Gospel of the grace of God, the unsearchable riches that are in Christ. Paul ends, as he began, and continued, with Christ Jesus our Lord, who is able to establish us in the fullness of the blessing of Christ.

About the Author

Robert C. McQuilkin (1886–1952) was the first president of Columbia International University from 1923-1952. In 1918, McQuilkin and his wife Marguerite were days away from an assignment as missionaries when the ship that was to carry them to Africa burned and sunk the day before the ship's departure. That left McQuilkin questioning God's next move for him and opened up the opportunity for McQuilkin to later accept the position to lead a new work in Columbia, South Carolina, called the Southern Bible Institute. It would soon be renamed Columbia Bible College, and by 1994, Columbia International University.

After earning a bachelor's degree from the University of Pennsylvania, McQuilkin began working in 1912 as associate editor for the influential *Sunday School Times*. It was during this period that McQuilkin established the Oxford Conference in Pennsylvania where he proclaimed the "Victorious Christian Life" message, which would become a core value of CIU.

In conjunction with CIU, McQuilkin founded the Ben Lippen Conference Center, a place where the Victorious Christian Life was proclaimed and where young people were encouraged to consider the mission field.

During his ministry, McQuilkin spoke widely and authored a number of books including, *The Lord is My Shepherd, Let Not Your Heart be Troubled, Victory in Christ,* and *Joy and Victory.*

CIU | Columbia International University

Columbia International University has proudly taken its place among the leading Christian universities and seminaries in America as we adapt with time and technology while staying true to our mission: CIU educates students from a biblical worldview to impact the nations with the message of Christ.

For more information about undergraduate, graduate and seminary programs at Columbia International University, visit www.ciu.edu

Scan this QR code with a smartphone to visit www.ciu.edu